Praise for *The Business of Being the Best*

"*The Business of Being the Best* unlocks valuable traits for the go-getters and change agents. The stories are compelling, the messages are clear, and passion for business and life comes through in every story. I hope millions read and get inspired!"

—**Edie Fraser**, senior consultant, Diversified Search

"*The Business of Being the Best* is a diamond mine of insight. Filled with gems from the world's most successful leaders, this invaluable guide will make your business glitter and your career shine."

—**Joey Reiman**, CEO, BrightHouse; author, *Thinking for a Living*

The Business of Being the Best

INSIDE THE WORLD OF GO-GETTERS AND GAME CHANGERS

Molly Fletcher

with Justin Spizman

Be Your BEST!

JOSSEY-BASS
A Wiley Imprint
www.josseybass.com

Published by Jossey-Bass
A Wiley Imprint
One Montgomery Street, Suite 1200
San Francisco, CA 94104-4594—www.josseybass.com

Library of Congress Cataloging-in-Publication Data

Fletcher, Molly.
The business of being the best : inside the world of go-getters and game changers / Molly Fletcher.—1st ed.
p. cm.
Includes bibliographical references and index.
ISBN 978-1-118-06010-0 (hardback); ISBN 978-1-118-15089-4 (ebk);
ISBN 978-1-118-15090-0 (ebk); ISBN 978-1-118-15091-7 (ebk)
1. Success. I. Title.
BF637.S8F5915 2011
650.1—dc23

2011034060

Printed in the United States of America
FIRST EDITION
HB Printing 10 9 8 7 6 5 4 3 2

To our daughters, Emma, Meg, and Kate
May you always be your best

Contents

Preface

For almost two decades, I have been a sports agent and worked with many of the biggest—make that legendary—names in sports. I didn't play professional baseball, or coach college ball, or even compete in a PGA Tour event, but even without those personal accomplishments on my résumé, I've succeeded at becoming America's leading and most recognized female sports agent in a male-dominated field.

Throughout my successful twenty-year career, I have worked with some of the most outstanding talents in the sports world. From baseball to basketball to golf and broadcasting where the elite play, I have been. I have helped lead my clients to success, and along the way, we've shared special moments on and off the field. They have become my friends, we've attended each other's weddings, many visited me in the hospital when my daughters were born, and we have shared our lives with one another. Having the opportunity to call world champions, future Hall of Famers, and headlining All-Stars my coworkers and friends has provided me with insight into the business of being the best.

I've had a successful career thus far, and CNN has even called me "the female Jerry McGuire," but I still feel I have much more to learn and achieve—and even more to give. I have never rested on my laurels. I take the same advice I give to my players every day: "No deposit, no return," just as it says on soft drink cans. What this phrase means is that you will get out of it what you put into it: make a big deposit, and you get a big return. Put in little effort, and you will find yourself with nothing. My clients have made huge sacrifices and deposits into their work to ensure that they achieve the best that they can. And I work hard to maintain the competitive edge that has allowed me to build a client base of over 150 clients and a team of agents.

For more than two decades, I have negotiated, directly and indirectly, over $500 million worth of contracts and pushed my clients to reach peaks even they could not have imagined. Working with the best day in and day out has helped me understand how they reach their full potential and maintain their place at the top of their respective arenas of business. I have shared the journeys of developing athletes, young coaches, rookie broadcasters, championship coaches, and prominent commentators. I have been exposed to a world of uniquely wonderful situations and have had a platform to connect with the world's best brands, best companies, best CEOs, and most successful executives on the planet—both in and out of the world of sports and the sports business.

The best can be any age and work in any profession. Certainly they are all very different, but they nevertheless carry a similar set of characteristics that push them to be top in their fields. By no means am I implying that any one of them is perfect—or even close to it. But they do share a common denominator that we can use to measure success: they measure their success by looking at their peers and their competitors. They work diligently to ensure that they are at the top of their respective industries. When it comes down to it, the go-getters and the game changers work to be considered one of the best by their peers and society at large.

At the heart of this book lies the fundamental idea that the best share a common set of traits and qualities that can be studied, copied, and instilled into your own life. There are individuals in our own lives whom we might call the best. The best teacher. The best boss. The best parent. Clearly, that is subjective. Some would argue that Michael Jordan is the best basketball player ever, but that also is subjective. So my goal is to share with you the less subjective side of what makes someone the best. In this book, I explain why the best do what they do, how they do it, and how you can learn from them, in the process transforming your professional life and joining the business of being the best. From the locker room to the boardroom, the playing field to the field of dreams, there are important lessons to learn.

Once you understand how the best view and approach their careers and their professions, you too will learn how to up your game, improve your business, and be your best. When you're at your best, not only do you define why you do what you do, but you also increase the success of those around you. People will naturally be attracted to you and to your mentality, ability, skills, and talents. In fact, not only will they want to work with you; they will also want to be around you.

In this book, I focus on some of the most important skills you will need to master in order to reach the top of your game. Whatever your industry may be, you will almost certainly find value in understanding how the best negotiate, relate to others, use their coworkers' strengths effectively, carry themselves, and maintain a high level of excellence throughout their careers.

The famous American journalist Marylin Vos Savant once said, "To acquire knowledge, one must study; but to acquire wisdom, one must observe." And from this point on, that is exactly what we will do. I have had the opportunity to not only study and observe the best but also to interview a cross-section of some of the most respected and accomplished athletes, coaches, businesspeople, philanthropists, and success stories. And through their stories, their experiences, and their insights, you will see what it takes to be the best.

I have kept the chapters in this book simple and tactical to ensure that you clearly understand how to implement these skills to improve your best traits. My goal is to help you succeed beyond your wildest imagination and reach goals you didn't even know you were capable of reaching. I want to help you create clarity and design a road map to reach your potential and navigate your way to extraordinary success.

No one becomes the best overnight, but when you read the last word in this book, you will have gained the knowledge you need to join the top 1 percent of go-getters and game changers in the world. You too will officially be on the road to being in the business of being the best.

Atlanta, Georgia
October 2011

Molly Fletcher

The Business of Being the Best

1

The Quest to Become the Best

Success is a journey, not a destination.
—Ben Sweetland

From the locker room to the boardroom, the practice field to the field of life, and the highlight reels to the business deals, the best are those who excel, succeed, and win both personally and professionally. They share a common set of traits and characteristics laced with passion and persistence that drives their success and fuels their inextinguishable flame. The best never stop striving for something far greater than the goals they have already reached. They never rest on their laurels, and they aim beyond the finish line. The finish line represents an end in sight, but the best see far beyond it to new possibilities. They understand the rapidity of change, and no matter how good they are, they always see room to improve.

What that tells us is that a critical core of a strong foundation, work ethic, intellect, persistence, and attention to details promotes a standard of excellence. Those who succeed in becoming the best work for every inch of success and accomplishment. An inch can be the difference in winning a game or losing it, and it is the same in business. The inches add up to the difference between where you are and where you want to be.

It is not luck or coincidence when you see a Major League Baseball (MLB) player hit a game-winning home run that sails over the outfield wall, a PGA golfer sinking the tournament-winning putt on the eighteenth hole, a coach leading his team to a world championship, or a CEO build a successful and profitable company out of his garage. These accomplishments are the result of diligent practice, dedication, and the hard work and determination it takes to get to the next level. The people who achieve these feats value hard work, are constantly fine-tuning their skills, and recover from adversity quickly. Their results come from consistently working hard at their trade.

Defining Your Own Version of Extraordinary

People who are the best in their field are relentless in their journey to become extraordinary. They have a strong desire to excel and succeed at what they do—selling, negotiating, hitting, kicking, throwing, or hosting. Why? They are competitive and love to win. And they want to win over and over again.

Through managing and working with the best, I have observed strong and experienced people fall from greatness, and I have seen newcomers rise to the pinnacle of record-breaking success. Although everyone has a unique path to achieving greatness, their stories, many of which I share in this book, are inspirational. We have all been told to try our hardest and do our best, and we all have our own definition of greatness. But it is possible to outperform even your own expectations and redefine your personal greatness to something more than you ever imagined. It is only by changing the way you think about success that you can fully embark on the quest to become the best.

In order to redefine your idea of personal greatness, begin by considering these questions:

- Why do you want to be the best?
- What does "being the best" mean to you in a year? Or in five years?
- How can you become the best?

Answering these questions will help you start your journey to becoming the best. The answers to some of these questions will come from within. Only you can decide why you want to be the best or what your inspiration is to improve and grow personally and professionally. But the stories surrounding the go-getters and game changers in this book will help you answer the question pertaining to how you can make it happen. Each of them has worked hard to become the best, and their insight and experiences will help you reach heights you have only imagined thus far.

Before you can hone your skills and refine your abilities, you have to build a strong foundation, so let's focus on the foundation that the best share. Through my work with successful executives and athletes, I have learned that all people who achieve extraordinary success in their field carry a set of similar qualities that enables them to put the rest in place. And the good news is that it's possible to learn from the best and apply their lessons in your own life and career. With a full understanding of these skills and characteristics, you will be able to grow into a successful businessperson, coach, community leader, entrepreneur, authority, doctor, lawyer, or future leader of your generation and generations to come.

We'll start this book by taking a look at what makes the best the best.

The Best Kick It Up a Notch

Being great means finding the top, and then kicking it up one or more levels. If you want to achieve greatness, you can't see ceilings, obstacles, or limitations as roadblocks. The best do not allow themselves to feel safe and comfortable; rather, they use every day as an opportunity to become a trailblazer and redefine success and the cutting edge. The most successful people in this world, no matter what area they are in, have a unique outlook on how they run their business, manage their employees, carve out niches, and manage their careers. Tom Izzo, head basketball coach of the Michigan State Spartans, missed an important free throw during his youth, and as a result, his team lost the game. To this day, Tom often finds time in his schedule to shoot and make fifty free throws a day. This kind of grit and intensity

Being great means finding the top, and then kicking it up one or more levels.

translate to success on the court and in his profession. Tom is now among the elite in his industry: he has won a National Collegiate Athletic Association (NCAA) championship, six Big Ten regular season titles, and two Big Ten tournament titles.[1]

Tom's dedication to being the best was clear in his behavior after his team won the national championship in 2000. Once the horn sounded the end of the game, he was cutting down the net, doing a media conference, and celebrating with his team and fellow coaches for hours. But he didn't bask in the victory for very long. The next morning he was already strategizing ways to persuade a recruit to come to Michigan State the next year. Tom could have relaxed and celebrated his success for a while, but he knew that if he was not focused on success in the future, his competitors would be. Kicking it up a notch means having a sense of urgency. Tom clearly has that.

Tony Conway, founder and owner of A Legendary Event, an award-winning special events company, said, "To be successful in business you need to have a taste for the unexpected . . . and an unending desire to make people happy." Tony has flourished and prospered as one of the leaders in the catering industry because he has a vision that few others have. He believes in the power of making people happy and that the most important part of his job is to create lasting and memorable experiences for his clients. His driving desire to be a groundbreaker in his industry is demonstrated in his attitude toward every event he puts on, and he has over twenty-five hundred of them every year. He believes that every guest who attends one of his events plays a vital role in his success. If he impresses each of them with his attention to detail and unexpected surprises, he will have one more sales rep pushing his product to the consumer industry—and that adds up to twenty-five thousand sales representatives around the country every year, who multiply the talents of his fifty employees in his company. He attends as many of his own events as possible.[2]

Tony has taken the concept of entertaining others to an entirely new level. He says that he separates his company from others by focusing his time and energy on making sure that the memories of the party will live forever in the minds of the guests. He meticulously studies every detail that goes into his events to ensure they are innovative and unmatched by anyone else in the industry. From something as small as the color schemes of a tablecloth to ensuring the band has the playlist that his client requested, no task is too big or too small for his attention. Understanding and anticipating what his customers want and need, sometimes even before they do, is the next level for him. Tony does that not only by being in the trenches himself but teaching others to see things the way he sees them, to solve problems the way he might, and to attend to his clients with the same vigor and passion that he does minute by minute. Tony surely would not be able to instill this level of customer service into his staff by sitting in a corner office on the top floor of a high-rise building. Tony exemplifies what I mean by going the extra mile, kicking it up a notch, and blowing the competition out of the water every day.

The best kick their momentum into high gear after they reach a milestone, as Tom did by starting his recruiting process the morning after his team won the national championship. They don't relax and pat themselves on the back when they accomplish something. When everyone else takes a break, they move forward. Once they have a taste of success, they want more and more and will work hard to get it. There is always more to be done, ways to improve, and higher goals to reach.

The best do not take their accomplishments for granted. They work hard to reach high levels of success, take great pride in their achievements, and find enormous pleasure in their triumphs. They hold on to the qualities that got them where they are and continue to build on their strong foundation.

The Best Adapt and Are Flexible

Game changers know that there are numerous routes to get to any destination, and sometimes they have to deviate from their planned path to achieve their desired results. Without the ability to adapt to changing circumstances, it is impossible to reach greatness. If you cannot be flexible when you encounter problems or difficulties that stand between you and your goal, you will never reach them. This is why the best make sure to adapt whenever the tide may turn.

When Roger Staubach, professional football player, Hall of Famer and Super Bowl Most Valuable Player quarterback, began Purcell High School in Silverton, Ohio, his coach, Jim McCarthy, immediately put Roger in the position of quarterback even though he previously had played various positions and had little experience as a quarterback. Nevertheless, he welcomed the opportunity. When asked why he made the change, McCarthy said that Roger's teammates listened to him, and the quarterback position would fit his strengths perfectly. Roger adapted to the position and excelled in it, and in the process, he learned at a young age that being flexible in life yields a number of advantages. Rather than fight the change to quarterback, he embraced it, and it led to a prosperous career as one of the best quarterbacks in National Football League (NFL) history. From a position change in football, to the jump from college football to the NFL, and the drastic change from retired NFL player to successful businessman, Roger has always been able to adapt.

It would have been easy for Roger to retire when his NFL playing days came to an end; he had, after all, been a football player his entire life. Instead he chose to adapt to the business world, and he built a business much like he had built a successful career as a football player: through hard work, dedication, and determination. In 1982, he founded the Staubach Company, a real estate development firm that he built from the ground up and sold in 2008 to Jones Lang LaSalle for several hundred million dollars. And he had a positive impact on a lot of lives along the way.[3]

In business as in the rest of life, things do not always go exactly how you plan. Detours and obstacles can close roads and force you to explore other paths. If you remain flexible and open, you will find endless opportunities to improve your life.

The Best Act As If They Have Been There Before

The best embrace success with anticipation. When they succeed, it appears as if they knew it was going to happen all along, whether or not they did. This reaction and attitude is part of what makes game changers so effective. Success doesn't come as a surprise to them because they always expect it, and even if they aren't completely certain of an outcome, they carry themselves with a confidence that makes others think they are.

This confidence supports future success because it instills trust in and inspires others. People want to work with those who are familiar with achievement and understand how to accomplish what they set out to do.

One of the greatest running backs in NFL history and a game changer, Barry Sanders, exemplifies this. Every time Barry touched the ball, it felt to him as if something amazing could happen, and often it did. Yet he retired before he broke every major rushing record. It was not that he didn't have it in him to break those records; rather, he felt that he had accomplished all he set out to do. For him, that was success. From an everyday perspective, the greatest accomplishment for a running back is scoring a touchdown. In fact, scoring more points than the other team is foundational to football. And Barry scored a whole lot of touchdowns in his nine-year career—109, in fact.[4] This is a staggering number of touchdowns for any position, especially in the ten years that he played professional football.

Barry will be remembered as a touchdown machine but never as a spectacle in the end zone. When he scored a touchdown, he did not celebrate or dance or pat himself on the back as most other players do. Rather, once he reached the goal line and proceeded into the end zone, he quietly and politely handed the ball to the referees. Tom Landry, a famous NFL football coach, once said, "Act like you have been there before." That was Barry's attitude. He was a running back and supposed to score touchdowns. He knew he belonged and expected to reach the end zone.

The same is true in business. The best are not surprised by their successes and truly believe that success will continue.

They hold themselves accountable and behave as if it would be strange if they were not successful. This attitude breeds success. I tell my clients that they should always strive to maintain a level of composure no matter what the situation. If they fail, they need to act as if it is only temporary—a speed bump in the road. And when they succeed, they should act as if this is not the first taste of success they have ever experienced. They should be grateful but believe in their ability to do it again.

Because a fair amount of emotion is involved in both athletics and business, it is natural and only human for athletes and top executives to react when they fail or succeed. But in our society, how you react to your successes and failures is just as important as whether you actually succeed or fail. Thaddeus Golas, a famous writer from the early twentieth century, said, "What happens is not as important as how you react to what happens." The best have all experienced exhilarating highs and plenty of lows too. Few successes, in fact, come without a series of disappointments and failures along the way—the inevitable bumps in the road. In fact, the failures actually help you succeed. How you react to these highs and lows is more telling of your character and heart than the height of the high or the depth of the low.

The best expect to hit the game-winning home run, or the last-second shot, or close the big business deal. They work for the promotion, but are not surprised when they receive it.

Acting as if you've been there before means keeping your composure and reacting to both successes and failures in a positive way. In fact, the simple act of maintaining composure can be the difference between success and failure. And even

How you handle success and failure can often be more important than the actual result.

more so, it can be the difference between succeeding and failing in the future because your reactions today influence how others perceive you and how they will think of you tomorrow. How you handle success and failure can often be more important than the actual result.

The Best Have a Two-Minute Memory

I tell athletes and coaches that when it comes to their success and failure, they need to have a short-term memory. Celebrate your accomplishments for two minutes, and dwell on your failures for two minutes, and no more. Less is okay. If you focus too much on your success, you can become complacent, and if you dwell too much on your failures, you can become fearful or depressed.

In 2008, one of my clients, MLB player Jeff Francoeur, was mired in one of the longest slumps of his career. He was tough on himself for his lack of success and could not dig his way out of it. He was playing for the Atlanta Braves, and the general manager at that time, Frank Wren, decided to demote Jeff to the minor leagues. After a home game, the coaches called him into the office and told him he would report to the minors effective immediately to work on his hitting. Jeff was upset and embarrassed, and felt as if he had let both himself and his team down. He called me on his way home from the ballpark at midnight, extremely disappointed. I listened and allowed Jeff to vent and share but then told him, "You have a choice right now, Jeff. You must embrace this. This is an opportunity to prove that you belong in the big leagues. Go down there and go three for four the first night with a home run and a couple of RBIs [runs batted in]." And then I put him on our corporate jet and sent him down to the minor league team.

Jeff did just what I told him: in three games, he had over a .500 batting average. And within three days, he was called back up to the majors. In 2010, Jeff played for the Texas Rangers when the team made it to the World Series. He had quickly grasped the concept of the two-minute memory during that tough run in 2008. After we spoke then, he knew he had no choice but to be upset for a few minutes, but then he had to move on. He could validate his failure or reinvent his success. The only solution was performing to the best of his ability, and Jeff did just that.

At some point, all of my clients and friends have dealt with challenges and even failure. Yet all of them knew that their failures were temporary, and they worked harder and longer to ensure it did not happen again. The reason they can do this is they do not dwell on their failures because if they do not have the right mind-set, they will not succeed. And so they quickly move on.

I've had this experience myself of failing and then embracing the experience to find success. In 1989 I was a freshman at Michigan State University rushing a sorority, playing great tennis, and enjoying college—until I got my grades for the first quarter and found out that my grade point average (GPA) was a

1.8, the lowest possible average a student could have while still being allowed to compete in sports. I had barely made the cut-off. My life was tennis. Had I not been able to compete, I would have been devastated. The experience scared me into ensuring that it would never happen again. I spent most of the rest of the year either in the library or on the tennis court and began to pull that 1.8 up to a respectable average. In fact, I received a 4.0 in all my classes the next semester and most of my classes for the rest of college, and I graduated with honors. I had recovered quickly. The failure had tested me and made me rise to the occasion.

So never spend too much time celebrating your wins or dwelling on your losses. Remember that the two-minute memory is just that: two minutes to celebrate and two minutes to dwell. Then you must move on with a positive attitude.

The Best Are Committed to Excellence

The best want to maximize their time on the world stage with the entire fabric of their being. Without this drive, they will not achieve extraordinary success. You will perfect the skills I set out in this book only if you are completely committed to being the best. You must be prepared to embrace greatness and distinction. The most successful people decide early on what their goals are, and their commitment to those goals remains steady and solid throughout life. Their commitment to excellence transcends any specific career path they may have. It is instead a way of life for them.

John Smoltz, a client and friend of mine of fifteen years, is a former Major League pitcher. For almost two decades, John was the definition of consistency and greatness on the field. He made eight All Star appearances and won the Cy Young Award in 1996, the highest honor a starting pitcher can receive. He almost certainly will be enshrined in the Hall of Fame. No doubt he is one of the best pitchers to play the game.

And off the field, he is a spiritual, classy, and outstanding role model for others. It was no mystery to his colleagues and coaches that he also had a knack for golf. After his playing days were over, John attempted to qualify for the U.S. Open Golf Tournament and become a professional golfer. In a field of over nine thousand, John fell just a few strokes short of making the cut and qualifying for the event on the Professional Golfers Association tour.

John was a Major League pitcher but he was so dedicated to excellence in all areas that he built golf holes in his back yard, spanning nine thousand square feet, so that he could focus on his golf game during his time off.

Just as in sports, the best in business have an inner fire that drives their commitment to excellence. While they may fall short of excellence at times, just as John did when attempting to qualify for the U.S. Open, it will never be because of their lack of dedication and desire to succeed.[5]

The Best Are Solution Architects

The best believe in solutions and possibilities, even in the face of a seemingly impossible problem or situation. They believe there is always a way and a means to reach their goals and solve their problems, and they find a way to put together the perfect solution. Life may place a huge obstacle in their path, but their first response is to find an alternative route. They focus their time on sketching solutions rather than succumbing to problems. No one has reached the pinnacle of success without dealing with numerous complications.

Arthur Blank, cofounder of Home Depot and owner of the NFL Atlanta Falcons, is widely considered to be one of the most successful businesspeople of our time, and he works hard to maintain that success. When Arthur bought the Falcons in 2002, a lot needed to be changed: winning more games and gaining community support, the quality of the practice facilities, and the parking for the game, to name just a few. Arthur had enormous issues to deal with, and if he wanted to succeed with the team, he knew that he would have to find creative solutions to them.

When training camp began, a friend near the practice field at Furman University offered Arthur a beautiful home to use. He greatly appreciated the offer but nevertheless declined: "I will stay in the dorms with the players, as I want to be close to the guys and see what they like and dislike about the facilities."

The first thing Arthur learned was that most players were sleeping on the floor: the mattresses were so thin that the floor was better. He also learned that they could barely get wet when taking a shower since the showerheads were too small for their frames. Because he experienced these issues personally, he clarified in his own mind the need for improved facilities for his players. Ultimately he moved the training facilities to Flowery Branch, outside Atlanta, and asked his players to pull together and tell him what they needed for success. Listening to the players and requesting their input in designing the new facility ensured the creation of a facility that everyone would be happy with, and it vastly improved morale.[6]

Another problem Arthur faced was at Georgia Dome, the stadium where the Atlanta Falcons play their home games. He learned quickly that the biggest complaint many of the fans had was the limited amount of parking surrounding the dome. Patrons who can't park easily stop buying tickets and attending games. So on one of his first days in his new office, Arthur strapped on his running shoes and walked four miles around the entire dome, plotting numerous new parking lots. And the result was that Arthur secured additional lots to house all of the cars he expected to see at Atlanta Falcons home games. As of 2011, the Atlanta Falcons have been surrounded with full parking lots for their sold-out games, welcoming over seventy thousand fans at each of the Falcons home games.[7] Arthur Blank has always taken great pride in his ability to acknowledge problems and quickly find creative and useful solutions.

The famous American educator Booker T. Washington once said, "Excellence is to do a common thing in an uncommon way." When it comes to finding solutions, this is the attitude of the best. Recognizing a problem is the easy part; finding a cost-effective, time-sensitive solution to that problem is what separates the good from the great. We all work under time and budget limitations, and the most successful people are those who use their time and budgets wisely. Whether you are the top CEO of a Fortune 500 company or an up-and-coming manager at a local business, you certainly will face problems. It will be your responsibility to find solutions to both easy problems and more difficult ones, like trying to figure out how to create parking for over seventy thousand fans attending a football game.

Regardless of what the issue is, the process involved in solving it remains the same: acknowledge the issue, envision a positive result, and think creatively about possible solutions, in the process being careful to not overcomplicate things, consider all the options, and choose the solution that is the most efficient and cost-effective while still delivering the necessary results. Throughout the entire process, keep a positive attitude and a steadfast belief that there is a solution out there, and you will find it.

Conclusion

Although there is not ever a single way to achieve success, go-getters and game changers all share the fundamental characteristics identified in this chapter that keep them driven and at the top. No matter what field you work in, you have to be intensely focused on working harder and smarter than all of your competitors to be the best. You have to adapt to the fluid landscape of your business. You have to welcome success and demonstrate a confident but humble attitude when it comes to both successes and failures. You have to commit yourself to excellence while remembering that how you respond to failure is just as important as how many victories you may have had. And finally, you have to be better at finding solutions than anyone else.

Understanding these traits and committing to developing and embracing them is your first step on the journey to being the best.

2

Negotiate Everything

In business, you don't get what you deserve, you get what you negotiate.
—Chester L. Karrass

Negotiating is not limited to those who make million-dollar deals to exchange goods or services. In fact, negotiating is the glue that holds our society together (or not). Negotiation is as basic and fundamental as doing a favor for a friend, asking your assistant to send out an important letter for you, or even making a large purchase at the local electronics store. In these situations, you are in a negotiation and may not even know it: you are negotiating that favor, service, or those goods. And the result of that or any other negotiation is based on how good you are at the process.

The best understand what negotiation is and how to do it. They are fully aware of its importance, so they spend a great deal of time and energy improving their negotiation skills.

Over the course of my career, I have negotiated over $500 million in contracts between my clients and sports teams, national and international companies, universities, and networks. I did not learn how to negotiate overnight. It has taken years upon years and negotiation upon negotiation to improve my skills so that I secure fair contracts, endorsements, and protection for my clients and my company. These are skills you can learn, and we will take a deeper look at those you need to have to obtain the best result. But before we move on to that it is vital for you to understand exactly where negotiation begins.

The Power of Asking

Every negotiation is different, but each starts with a single fundamental act: asking a question. You can't begin the process of negotiating until it is clear what all the involved parties want from it, and the only way to find out is to ask. This question could be about what another party is looking for from a deal, for example, or what your client wants to gain. Sometimes the other side may not even know you are starting the negotiating process. You may just be testing the waters with questions to see if negotiation is something you want to pursue. But whether or not the other side is aware that you are opening the channels of negotiation, you need to ask those on the other side what they are looking for if you plan to get anywhere. The most successful closers know that before they can start negotiating, they need insight from the other party to figure out if that other party needs what you have to offer.

The following story truly illustrates the power of asking a question to see if there is a need. In 1990, Star 94, a radio station in Atlanta, Georgia, was giving away prizes, and the winner was a seventeen-year-old young man. He went to the station to pick up his prize and saw Tom Sullivan, a popular nighttime DJ, in the lobby. The young man struck up a conversation with Tom and explained that he had won a prize and was there to pick it up. He went on to say that he attended a local high school and listened to Tom's show. He then asked if he could have a tour of the radio station. Tom gave the teenager a tour and showed him the DJ booth. The young man was dazzled and fascinated and told Tom that he would love to watch him do his show sometime. In return, he'd be happy to provide any help the station might need.

This fan was interested in becoming a DJ and came back repeatedly to see Tom do the nighttime show. Eventually he started helping out and then answering phones. After a few months of this, Tom invited him to a Star 94 client party where about 150 to 200 clients were in attendance. In fact, Tom not only invited him but asked him to be the host. So when this young man walked onto the stage in front of a room full of people, he began by greeting the guests: "Welcome everyone! I am Ryan Seacrest."

All of the top executives from the radio station were confused; they had no idea who this kid was and didn't know that none of the regular DJs were available to host the event that evening, so Tom had volunteered Ryan. After the initial shock that a seventeen year old was hosting an event for numerous clients wore off, the president of the radio station realized that the evening's emcee was the teenager who had been hanging on Tom Sullivan's coattails for the past few months and that he had enormous potential. As Ryan hosted the event, he captivated and charmed the audience, and most station executives were overwhelmed with both curiosity and amazement at how good he was on stage.

Even at the young age of seventeen, he was the same as he is today, an amazing talent. From that night on, Ryan returned to the station and was eventually hired to do the weekend shifts. The summer after his senior year in high school, Ryan worked as a full-time radio DJ until he eventually went to school at the University of Georgia. However, he would return every weekend to host the night shifts until he realized his calling was in California and eventually made his way to Los Angeles.[1] Shortly after, Ryan was chosen to be the host of the widely popular television show *American Idol.* He has hosted this show since 2002 and now has his own syndicated radio and television show.

Seacrest has become a tremendously successful media personality, and his career started with a question: "Can I take a tour of your radio station?" That single question sparked one of the most successful careers in entertainment today. Whether or not he realized it, Ryan was negotiating. Through his questions, he negotiated a tour, a mentor, a position in the nighttime show, and ultimately the experience he needed to take the next step in his own career.

Negotiations aren't just an exchange of goods or services for money. Star 94 gave Ryan experience and an opportunity, and with his eagerness to learn, Ryan gave Star 94 not only free help but eventually a fantastic DJ for their radio station.

On that first day in the Star 94 office, Ryan negotiated his way into one of the most valuable things anyone can negotiate for: an opportunity.

The Value of Negotiation

Ryan's story shows that negotiations can end in enormous success and opportunity. He may not have realized at the time that he was negotiating, but rest assured, he was.

The power of negotiation cannot be understated. Each of us has boundaries, constraints, and limitations that prevent us from agreeing to any offer we receive. Negotiating is an opportunity to maximize our own outcomes and also to ensure we are not taken advantage of. Negotiating can give you an opportunity, improve your situation, add to your bottom line, or even change your life. I have negotiated hundreds of deals, but I remember one of my own life-changing negotiations as if it was yesterday.

Negotiating can give you an opportunity, improve your situation, add to your bottom line, or even change your life.

In 1993 I moved to Atlanta after college. I packed my Honda Accord with most of my belongings, left my home in Michigan, and headed south to start my career. I had two thousand dollars to my name, which I had saved from my summer jobs, which was not very much even in 1993. The best I could tell, I had about two months of security. When I arrived in Atlanta, my first goal was to find a place to call home, which would be difficult with my meager finances. But one thing I did know was how to market myself and fight for a good deal.

Before I had left Michigan, my tennis coach provided me with a few names of people in Atlanta to contact for networking purposes. But when I called those people, they all said some sort of variation of this: "You know, tennis is a big deal in

Atlanta, and there are some apartment complexes in Atlanta where you can teach tennis in exchange for your rent."

With this information in mind I drove to the nicest apartment complexes throughout the city and knocked on the leasing office's doors and asked for the manager. I would say, "I noticed you had tennis courts in your complex. I wanted to inquire whether you have a tennis pro." I quickly found out that not only did most of these complexes have a pro, but the pros had been working for the complexes for numerous years. But I did not give up. In fact, the complex I had my eye on was near a local pizza shop, Pero's Pizza. I stopped by the restaurant after I left the apartment complex and asked for the manager or owner. A few minutes later, Charlie Pero walked to the front of the restaurant. I said, "Hello, I am new to the area, and I have a somewhat random question for you. Do most of your customers come from a few miles of this restaurant?" He replied, "Why, yes, why?" I told him that I was possibly going to be teaching tennis across the street and wondered if he would provide me with a dozen or so free pizzas once a month for the residents from the property who attend my tennis clinics. I said I thought I could add information or coupons for Pero's Pizza in the apartment complex's newsletter. He paused and said, "Sounds great. Can you pick them up or do you want them delivered? You can just let me know what folks want on the pizza and give me a day or so notice. That sounds great!" Next thing I knew he was showing me the kitchen and introducing me to his wife, the cooks, and the delivery folks. I quickly swung back by the apartment complex and said to the manager I had spoken to earlier, "So sorry to bother you, but I did want to let you know that I chatted with the owner of a nearby pizza place, and I have arranged for pizza to be delivered monthly as part of my tennis clinic for the residents to enjoy. I thought we could add a little information about the restaurant in your newsletter." She smiled hesitantly and said, "That's great, but as I said, we have a pro." I confidently smiled and replied, "Great, let me know if something changes, I'm ready."

I followed up with each complex as well as the tennis pros whom I had connected with. Through the grapevine, I had learned the complex I was stalking was about to find out that its pro was leaving.

As a result, I stopped by the complex one morning again and said to the manager, "Hey, I am sorry to bother you again, but I have another idea for you." She smiled. Since I knew her primary goal as a manager was to fill those apartments as well as differentiate her complex from others in the surrounding area, I said, "I can help you fill these apartments by positioning the tennis program as a real amenity. What is your occupancy now?" She told me the complex was not full, so I explained how we could use tennis to differentiate the complex from the surrounding ones. The apartment complex was in a highly competitive location, with thousands of new units being built each year. So with this increasing competition for tenants, I told her I would call my contacts at Wilson Sporting Goods to do promotions and giveaways for current residents. This, I told her, would help raise occupancy and make her look like a hero to her boss and the owners.

She considered what I had said and then responded, "Your persistence has paid off," and she told me that her tennis pro had just informed her that he was getting married and moving out. She said, "I can do for you what I did for him." She could offer me $350 off the rent of a standard $850 apartment to teach lessons one evening a week. I would make up the $500 difference with a check to the complex every month. But I took it further: "I will help you fill these apartments with tenants who bring friends to my clinics who may also decide to rent your apartments. And they will love the clinics so much they will want to move in or renew their leases."

I knew the manager liked my ideas and me, so I kept pushing: "I would love to help you, but I really would need the entire rent waived. So let's get this place full of tenants." I stopped talking, smiled, and looked at her. She said, "What?" I replied, "Trust me. We can do magical things with your occupancy. I'll be your second sales rep. Be my agent; sell it to your owner. The apartment is empty anyway, and I can fill up the other empty ones. Just put a roof over my head, and I will make you look like a hero. I promise. My pizza guys are ready, Wilson is in. I can even write tennis tips in our complex newsletter [notice the word *our*] for the residents." She smiled and replied, "All right. Let me check with my boss. I'll see if I can get her on the phone."

I stopped her before she walked into her office to call her boss and said, "Hey, thank you. I wouldn't push this if I didn't think I could really help you." She made the call to her boss and about twenty minutes later came out and said to me, "It is done: a one bedroom with no rent in exchange for teaching one two-hour tennis clinic a week. I will have someone show you some of the apartments that are open, and you can pick the one you like, move in, and start next week."

I thanked her, and said, "No need to spend time on the tour. I'll take the one-bedroom unit closest to the tennis court." After that day, I got pizza donations and sponsors and ran a successful tennis clinic out of the apartment complex. I was even asked to be the pro for a neighboring complex with the same owners when their tennis pro left as well, expanding the clinic from one tennis court to five tennis courts. More courts created additional revenue streams. And it all started with a simple negotiation.

Never underestimate your power in negotiating. Through pushing my position and working hard to demonstrate how I could add value, I negotiated my way into a position and eventually built a small clinic among the apartment complexes, creating additional income by coaching organized leagues out of the property, along with free rent. I was successful during this negotiation because I supported my position and demonstrated how I could make a difference to the apartment complex. Demonstrating persistence, resources, work ethics, smarts prior to the deal helped as well. I spent almost a decade in a free apartment working my way up in the sports business while eliminating a large monthly fixed expense.

In any negotiation, it is vital to your success to illustrate that you will help the other person. No one wants to leave a negotiation feeling as if he or she got a raw deal or got the short end of the stick. I promised results and I delivered those results, justifying the leasing agent's decision to go to bat for me. But it all started with a goal in mind and a desire to achieve that goal through hard work.

The value of negotiation is often found in the end result. In the end, we all benefited; I got free rent and, by being proactive and creative, added value to the apartment complex beyond what was generally expected of the average tennis pro. But to get there, I had to step up, be diligent, and not give up on the negotiation process.

The Three D's of Negotiation

Always start a negotiation by asking yourself four fundamental questions:

1. Is there a need?
2. What can I offer the other side?
3. What can the other side do for my client or me?
4. What is the benefit of entering into this negotiation?

The story of my rent-free apartment in Atlanta illustrates the most fundamental techniques of a negotiation. I call it the three D's of negotiation: discover the need, demonstrate you have a solution, and deliver your solution. That is the fundamental basis for any negotiation. And once you implement these concepts into your negotiations, whether in an attempt to obtain a better price on purchasing a new television or trying to close a multimillion-dollar contract, you will put yourself in a better place to succeed.

Discover

With any negotiation, the first and possibly most crucial step to a successful outcome is discovering exactly what the other side is looking for. When I negotiated a rent-free deal in Atlanta, my first step was to get inside the mind of a leasing agent and gain an understanding as to what supports her success. Within minutes, I discerned that she wanted to please her boss and illustrate that she could make decisions to increase profitability and fill empty apartments.

If you have a fundamental understanding of what the other side would like to achieve when you begin any negotiation, you are ahead of your competition. Sometimes this can be easy. In my situation, it was not difficult to understand that a leasing agent's main goal is to put tenants in the apartments. And once I found out that the complex was in need of a tennis pro, I knew I could help. It was through my diligence and consistent follow-up that I discovered that the previous tennis pro had left and that this kind of amenity was considered a value in area apartment complexes. In other situations, discovering the other side's goals through negotiating may not be as easy. Once you discover exactly what the other side wants or needs, you can begin the next step: formulating a strategy to demonstrate how you can fit their need.

Demonstrate

My second goal was to demonstrate how I could fit the need for a new tennis pro. It was also my responsibility to demonstrate that the apartment owners would be better with me than without me. Obviously my experience as a collegiate athlete helped my cause, but I went even further: I demonstrated that in addition to teaching tenants how to improve their tennis game, I could use my skills in a creative manner to market, advertise, and promote the apartment complex in creative ways.

In any negotiation, you have to be able to demonstrate that you have the ability to solve the problem or address the need. Furthermore, you have to demonstrate that the other party would be crazy not to close the deal with you.

If, when you are negotiating, you can demonstrate that you have strategically thought through the other side's goals, you will gain an inside track into closing the deal. People respond to solutions, and it is your responsibility to illustrate that you have the know-how and ability to deliver.

Deliver

Finally, it is easy to talk the talk, but real negotiators walk the walk. If you cannot deliver on your promises, all of this effort is for naught. When negotiating with the leasing agent, I told her I could deliver Wilson as a supporter for giveaways and events and support the apartment owners' efforts to increase occupancy. Furthermore, I promised I could deliver free pizzas for our events. If I came back later to apologize for not delivering these promises, I bet I never would have closed the negotiation with free rent.

Shortly after we agreed on terms, I delivered on these promises, ranging from small things like pizzas to calling a potential tenant to explain the tennis program. I worked hard to create a more involved and engaged community through offering tennis clinics and tennis teams.

It is my firm belief that you should always overperform. Whenever I negotiate, I always make promises I am confident I can deliver on. And I did just that during my years at the property: the apartment complex continuously outperformed its competition, in part due to tennis being a successful and appealing amenity. There is no benefit to proposing solutions that you cannot deliver on, and if you do promise something and fall short, the relationship and the deal will fall apart before you know it. So it is always better to underpromise than underperform. You will always be held accountable, and if you don't perform, you will lose the trust and respect of those you are negotiating with, and they will have no desire to work with you again.

Attributes of a Successful Negotiator

Gaining a basic understanding of negotiating is key to succeeding in any negotiation, but that is just one piece of the pie. In addition to discovering, demonstrating, and delivering, there are three basic characteristics that will help you win over the other side before the negotiations even begin. Think about the type of people you want to surround yourself with. Chances are they are trustworthy, you can relate to them, and they are sensitive to your needs and the needs of those around them. Therefore, when I am negotiating, I always focus on relaying three basic qualities to the other side: trustworthiness, rapport, and awareness. If those on the other side believe you, relate to you, and feel you are aware of their needs, they will be open to negotiation and more receptive to your needs and desires. People have a lot of choices today when it comes to making deals, so if you want to regularly close deals, you need to have a professional, mutually respectable relationship with those on the other side of the negotiation.

When I am negotiating, I always focus on relaying three basic qualities to the other side: trustworthiness, rapport, and awareness.

Trustworthiness

If people don't believe you, they will avoid negotiating with you. Negotiations work best when the other party feels safe and comfortable. This means they feel that they can share their concerns, issues, and challenges, along with anything else that is holding them back, because they trust that you will be responsive to them, and they know that you will be empathetic to their issues and not take advantage of the information they freely have offered for your own gains. They need to know that they are not being cheated, so you must be prepared to support what you say and say only things that you can support. Trust is built when the statements you make become a reality. It is no mystery that if the people with whom you are negotiating feel as if they are being taken advantage of, the negotiations will come to a sudden and quick halt. And generally that will be the last time you deal with those people.

Mark Twain once said, "If you tell the truth, you don't have to remember anything." One bad or dishonest negotiation can break the trust of a thousand good ones. It destroys your credibility. Whereas it can take years upon years and deals upon deals to gain the trust of your peers, it takes only one untrustworthy or underhanded act to tear that trust apart.

Rapport

Rapport is easy to define but hard to obtain. It is a combination of being respectful, being sincere, and having the ability to relate to others. When you can communicate with those you are negotiating with in a respectful manner, demonstrating that you are sincerely involved in and committed to the process, people will be attracted to both you and the position you are representing. Rapport is something that has to be built, and you need to be aware that from the moment you walk into a negotiation, you are either building rapport through your actions and behaviors or sabotaging it.

As a young woman, I walked into the office of the general manager of the Braves, John Schuerholz, to negotiate John Smoltz's contract. At the time, John Schuerholz and I had a friendly and mutually respectable business relationship, but there was certainly still room for it to be closer. As I entered his office, his computer screen faced the entry door and the screen saver was on the famous par three hole number twelve at Augusta National, the golf course that hosts the Masters tournament. As I pointed to his screen, I said, "What did you get on number twelve last time you played?" He swung his head around and said, "I parred it." I humbly and somewhat softly said, "Nice. I birdied it." He smiled genuinely and said, "Nice job." A lot of little messages were being sent during that short exchange, and the result was an closer rapport.

Rapport is magnetic. Once you've built it with someone, that person will be attracted to your presence and have an inexplicable yet pleasant affinity toward working with you. Finding similarities, or a rapport, with those on the other side is how you gain trust in a negotiation. The similarities, the likability, the common ground, and the sincere and respectful manner are all part of building the rapport that lays the foundation for trust. Working together strengthens it, but without the foundation of strong rapport, you will stand no chance of building the trust you need to succeed as a negotiator over the long run.

Awareness

Being aware of the needs and wants of those with whom you are negotiating is vital to your success as a negotiator. If you are aware of the other side's needs, you can anticipate how they will act or react. And knowing their next move is extremely valuable. Imagine a negotiation to be like a game of chess. You always have to think a couple of moves ahead and constantly ask yourself, "What is the other side thinking about? What do they really want? What do they really need and why? What will they do next?" If you know the answer to these vital questions, you will have responses and reactions ready before the move is even made. This response not only helps you to be prepared and appear credible but also shows those you are negotiating with that you are aware of exactly what it is they are attempting to gain.

Concepts That Work Together

Trust, rapport, and awareness: these three seemingly separate concepts work together to build a strong foundation for every negotiation process. Once you are aware of the needs of the person with whom you are negotiating, it is easier to demonstrate a sincere desire to help fill those needs, thereby building rapport. When this happens, those on the other side will warm up to you and will be more likely to open up and communicate honestly with you, creating a strong trust. The awareness and rapport simply aid in building that trust. Once you obtain another's trust, that person will not only want to work with you but will want to work for you. He or she will endeavor to help you fill your own needs so that you reach a mutually beneficial outcome.

Preparing to Negotiate

Before you begin the negotiation process you need to prepare by creating a blueprint for that specific negotiation. In order to be successful in any negotiation, you must win the trust of those you are hoping to do business with. Of course, being trustworthy isn't enough. You also need to know what you're talking about. Three main factors will help you prepare a blueprint for a negotiation: understanding the big picture, understanding what motivates the other side, and understanding what factors are within your control and what factors are not.

Understanding the big picture means that you need to do background research so that you can speak knowledgably about the issues at hand. Having an understanding of what motivates the individual or group of individuals you want to do business with helps you design a creative and effective plan that will meet both their needs and yours and cater to their specific desires and situation. By being realistic about what factors you can control and what factors you can't (what I call *inside factors* and *outside factors*), you are prepared for all possible questions, difficulties, and obstacles.

As a sports agent, I negotiate on two levels: for the clients and with the clients. Before I have the honor to call a professional athlete a client, I have to earn his or her trust and friendship. These athletes can choose from many agents in the industry to negotiate their contracts and endorsements. (In fact, in some sports, there are more registered agents than there are athletes to represent.) I have to negotiate with them before I can ever negotiate for them. As part of my job, I pitch these athletes, coaches, and broadcasters constantly. We speak over the phone, meet in person, and discuss their future more times than you could imagine before they hire me to represent them. This process always starts with good planning.

Before I speak to them, I make sure I know my potential client's history, current situation, and, as much as possible, what he or she is looking for in the future. I gather data and familiarize myself with them. I anticipate the potholes in the negotiation process and work hard to ensure that I have thought about these obstacles and have answers for each of them. And I consider all potential issues and questions so that when the negotiations begin, I have run through all the possibilities fully, understand my goal, and have a clear vision as to how I will get there.

If you do not create a blueprint, you are entering blindly into the process and are lowering the odds of a positive outcome from the start, especially if you are competing against others who have done their homework. Whenever you enter a negotiation process, the desired outcome is success in, say, closing a great business deal or acquiring a new home. Whatever it is, proper planning is the key to your success. When you prepare, you arm yourself with the knowledge that will help you avoid the pitfalls and obstacles that so many people fall victim to in the negotiation process. There is nothing worse than leaving a negotiation and saying to yourself, "I should have seen that coming." That is what blueprinting helps prevents.

Understand the Big Picture

"Understanding the big picture" means that you have to know what your ultimate goal is, what their ultimate goal is, and how you will achieve it. It is vital to your success as a negotiator. The best way to start understanding the big picture is to gather all the data that you can.

Some general information about your potential client—his or her needs, desires, future goals, strengths, and weaknesses—will help you quickly gain a general understanding as to what this person is looking for from this relationship. In my field, without knowing a potential client's stats, career history, and background, how would I ever be able to effectively represent him or her?

Since this information is so vital to the success of a negotiation, count on spending a great deal of time and effort to gather and analyze it to ensure that you are properly prepared and truly do understand the big picture. The good news is that we live in an era where information and data are readily available. When I pitch a new client, I scour the Internet to find as much as I can about that person's past, current situation, and relationships. I also consider what relationships we may have in common. Do we have mutual friends? Are or were they teammates with a client? Business colleagues we have both worked with? Nothing is too minor to be overlooked. Only when you understand the person or group you are dealing with can you sculpt a strong plan that will help you reach your desired end result.

Understanding the Motivation

Everyone has a reason for negotiating. Sure, all negotiations are focused on a specific deal or outcome, but why does your potential client want to reach that deal? What exactly does she have to gain by coming to terms with you? And what is she willing to be flexible (or inflexible) about? What is so important to her that she is willing to sacrifice something else?

To become a successful negotiator, you have to gain insight and understanding into what motivates the other half of the negotiation. The entire point of a negotiation is for two sides to come together to create one mutually beneficial result. Before you begin negotiating, you will surely understand your own motivating factors, but knowing what motivates the other side is not as easy.

So what is it that motivates your potential partner? What is important to her? Is it money? Is it location? Something more? Proximity to family and friends, the types of endorsements he will do, or the culture a specific city may offer are all concerns and motivating factors. And even the smallest concerns become big when it is time to sign a long-term deal. An athlete may be willing to take a smaller salary if it means moving to a city that is a comfortable place for his family. So taking the time to understand what motivates the player before blindly diving into a negotiation can make all the difference. It means I can offer him what he wants, as opposed to what I think he wants.

This holds true for any negotiation you may be part of. You have to know whom you are dealing with. If you cannot answer fundamental questions about your position or that of the other side, as well as that person's desires and motivating factors, your ability to succeed drops.

When I was negotiating a deal for a Major League Baseball (MLB) player, Mark DeRosa, my team's preparation made the difference between a good deal and a great for him. Mark was a good player, but when he was playing for the Atlanta Braves, he was not yet known as a star player. I had recruited and signed him early in 2000 in part due to his friendship with some of my other clients. After this season, Mark was set to become a free agent. However, MLB teams usually hold players' rights for a period of time after the season ends. I knew the Braves were going to do this with Mark, even though we were confident they had no plans to offer him a contract based on the team's current needs. So we approached the Braves and asked the team to release Mark so we could get a head start on free agency. We knew that there were twenty-nine other teams that presented better odds for playing time for Mark than the Braves could offer. Based on our relationship with the organization and continued push, the Braves released Mark early, which gave us extra time.

A lot of teams were interested in Mark; however, after flying to meet with Buck Showalter and gaining confidence that the Texas Rangers was the best fit, Mark signed with the team. He achieved incredible numbers during that year with the Rangers, laying the foundation for the Chicago Cubs deal we negotiated for Mark the next year: a three-year, $13 million contract. Our preparation and efforts in getting him an early release and then studying the market to get him to the right team laid a strong foundation for this career-making contract.

The big picture was that we needed to get out of Mark's current deal so we could beat other free agents to the teams who needed a player with Mark's skill set. We knew there were numerous teams that needed to sign a second baseman who could play multiple other positions. We knew as well that if we could get Mark to free agency, he could sign quickly and have a chance to start for a team instead of sitting on the bench. Our hopes were that if he played well, we could set him up for a huge deal the next year. Understanding the big picture and looking past the next season enabled us to set Mark up for a multimillion dollar contract. We knew the Rangers needed a second baseman and were not afraid to bet on Mark, so we jumped at that opportunity. Understanding the big picture and studying our audience's motivation led us, throughout his career, to over $25 million in contracts for Mark.

When you put the time and effort into preparing for any negotiation, you not only put yourself or your client in a place to succeed; you almost certainly will have the upper hand on the competition. Without proper planning, you will almost surely crash and burn.

Understanding the Inside and Outside Factors of Negotiation

In addition to understanding the big picture and the motivating factors of those involved, I also ensure that before any negotiation, I study the difference between the inside and outside factors. The inside factors are those that are directly related to your client or your position in the negotiation process; these could be anything from your bottom line to your strengths and weaknesses. The outside factors are the ones you may not have control over but are directly linked to your negotiable position and will certainly have an effect on the end result. For example, if you are negotiating for a contract but are competing against other companies that also want that contract and your competitors have more money to spend on advertising, marketing, or research, you simply have no control over that. But it is important to be aware of your competitor's position so that you can focus on those factors you can control to ensure you outsmart them. You can always make up for any uncontrollable financial or other lack with creative thinking and hard work. Understanding factors that you cannot control will often allow you the opportunity to counteract the outside factors with inside factors.

You never know what factors will become the tipping point of a negotiation. Negotiations are like riding a seesaw: they can tip with just a little shift in weight. So it is vital to have a fundamental awareness and understanding of each of these elements so you can control the shift.

The Inside Factors

You have control over a significant part of the negotiation. Here are a few examples:

- You control your preparedness and attention to detail, how you communicate, how you present your ideas, how you react to others and their ideas, and much more.
- You choose how you value and prioritize what is being negotiated.
- You can decide to accept deal points during the process or reject them.

All good negotiators control as many variables as they can to strengthen their chances of getting a good deal.

All good negotiators control as many variables as they can to strengthen their chances of getting a good deal.

Before any negotiation, consider what inside factors you can manage and mold to ensure they are working for you. Preparation, accountability, attention to detail, and how you choose to communicate during the negotiation are just a few of these inside factors. I have successfully negotiated numerous deals, and I attribute many of these positive results to my attention to the factors that I can control and my understanding of those that I cannot. By making sure the factors within your control are in perfect order, you can spend time preparing to answer questions around those that you cannot control, which will put you light-years ahead of your competitors in the race to close the deal.

Consider the following inside factors that you can control or define.

Your Bottom Line You have to understand exactly what your reasons for negotiation are. What are you trying to achieve or obtain? Essentially you have to ask yourself, "What is my bottom line? What do I want?" If you do not have a strong grasp of the basic reasons that you are spending time going back and worth with the other side, it will be almost impossible to achieve your goals. You need to understand what you absolutely must get from this process but also what you are willing to let slide in order to reach your ultimate goal.

Before I enter into any negotiation process, I sit down with my clients and gain clarity from them regarding our bottom line and our expectations. This conversation creates focus and helps us to stay the course and focus on what is important, while letting the not-so-important things go by the wayside.

Your Strengths and Weaknesses What is working in your favor? What isn't? You need to be fully aware of your strengths and your weaknesses and be prepared for conversations regarding both. If I have a player who performs better against right-handed pitching than left or a broadcaster who calls baseball games better than football games or a coach whose win-lose record is poor, I am going to anticipate the conversation that may surface concerning that negative performance. It is almost like a strategic strike. If you know you are up against a potential issue, it is in your best interest to prepare to discuss that issue as if it will be the center of the entire negotiation. That way, when it rears its ugly head, you will be ready to face it and demonstrate to the other side exactly why that is not nearly as big of an issue as it may seem. You then need to steer the conversation toward what you can offer and away from what you can't. The ability to focus on strengths and minimize weaknesses comes from processing knowledge and facts through razor-sharp preparation and effective anticipation.

Your Big Picture What you do today will affect what will happen tomorrow. You cannot make decisions or act in a vacuum. You have to take into account your big picture. Don't focus only on the opportunity before you but also its effects on your long-term goals. If you don't keep the big picture in mind, you could make a decision that you will later regret.

I represent a significant number of professional golfers, and one day a large company that produces golf clubs and golf balls (among other products) approached me with a lucrative deal for one of my clients. However, once my client practiced with these clubs, he discovered that he did not like the equipment and that it had an adverse effect on his overall performance. Since the opportunity to obtain this endorsement came from his success on the course, if he used the clubs and could not maintain this success, he would be in no position to receive future endorsements. Together we decided to turn down this deal since we knew that the clubs would not be a good fit for him.

We could have easily taken the money and run. But after the two-year deal expired, if these clubs did in fact have a negative effect on my client's performance, we could be sacrificing millions in on-course earnings and endorsements, not to mention his livelihood as a professional golfer.

You always have to focus on the big picture. Every decision you make while negotiating creates a domino effect that can change your course forever.

Your Communication You have complete control over how you choose to communicate with potential business partners. There is no excuse to lose a deal because of your communicative approach. Does the other side seem to connect with your message? Is this person engaged and listening? If not, you need to adjust what you're saying, when you are saying it, or how you're saying it. You may need to tailor your communicative style to your audience, so pay attention to how your potential client is reacting to you.

Your Presentation Regardless of what your ideas are, how you present them is a key factor in your success. When you present your ideas, you are essentially pitching your product, your business, and certainly yourself. It is imperative that you introduce this information to the other side in the best possible way. To get your potential business partners to buy into you and your ideas, you have to offer a detailed and comprehensible game plan. Be creative, be clear, and be prepared.

Your Accountability Having a reputation for accountability is important in all business relationships, and certainly when it comes to negotiating. It is one thing to take accountability for your successes, but another thing entirely to accept accountability when things go wrong. If you are perceived as someone who places blame rather than accepts responsibility, you will be hard-pressed to find people willing to do business with you or even consider negotiating with you. If, however, you demonstrate that you are accountable for the things you say and do, as well as your successes, people will trust that when things go wrong, you will be the first to stand up, apologize, and diligently work to fix the issue. This stance will make it much more likely that other parties will enter into a negotiation and relationship with you.

Your Reactions In any negotiation, you always have control over how you react to any given situation. Do you appear nervous? Scared? Angry? Frustrated? Any of these emotions will likely be clear to your potential business partner, and none of them will help your cause. Your reactions should never be overly emotional, regardless of whether those emotions are positive or negative.

Think about what your reactions reflect to the other side and what feelings may arise from that reaction. Your reacting to something negatively will put the other side off and make them question the wisdom of entering into the negotiation. And if you jump excitedly at something they offer and are overly eager, they may use that to take advantage of you. Stay humble, stay focused, and stay committed to ensuring your reactions are even.

It is human nature to get emotional during a negotiation. Nevertheless, prepare yourself for the emotions that might arise during the discussion and remain aware of them throughout the process so that you can keep them in check.

Your Appearance Unless you have a track record in business that is unmatched, it is imperative that you are well dressed and look professional. Clearly, being aware of how the other party is likely to react to your appearance is relevant. Your appearance should always mirror and complement your potential business partner or be a slight step up. This may seem obvious, but in my hundreds of negotiations, I have seen anything and everything. I always consider who my audience may be on any given day and dress appropriately for that audience. Looking professional will work in your favor.

Your Attention to Detail Everything had better be perfect, from the first capital to the last. When it comes to written communications, accuracy is key. A lack of accuracy may be interpreted in many different ways, and none of them will help your position. Your attention to detail is a reflection of you and your work. If you do not reread your e-mails, focus on the small details, or fine-tune your presentations, your potential business partner will most likely wonder what else you gloss over. You should always be proud of your work and confident in your product, and it all starts with concentrating and focusing on the details.

Your Desire to Close the Deal Do they know you want to consummate the deal? Is it evident? I sure hope it is. If you are not sending positive messages about the end game, no one else will be either. One way to show your desire and that you're committed to closing a deal is through genuine enthusiasm and curiosity about the possibilities. But be careful, because desire is a balancing act. You have to show motivation and strong interest in getting the deal done, but being overly anxious or overzealous can hurt your negotiating position. There is a fine line between being enthusiastic and desperate. Let them know you'll do what it takes to close the deal, but don't let them think your life or your business depends on it.

A Bright Idea All great negotiators use inside factors to their advantage. They understand not only what they are but also how they can play an integral part in the negotiation process. Joey Reiman, the founder and CEO of BrightHouse, a company that works with many Fortune 500 companies to formulate ideas to fuel their marketing and advertising campaigns, is a go-getter and a brilliant negotiator. His life's work provides numerous examples of how one person has taken these inside factors and repeatedly influenced them to successfully negotiate.

Joey Reiman thinks for a living and has been the driving force behind some of the most successful ad campaigns in American history. He is a master of the pitch, and to land some of these coveted accounts, he consistently thinks creatively. He differentiates his company from the rest with his attention to detail, outstanding communicative practices, and the ability to create positive emotions in and gain excellent reactions from his potential clients. He is a master negotiator and makes a point to truly understand the needs of those he negotiates with.

When his company was vying for the $50 million account of Del Taco, a Mexican-American fast food restaurant, Joey was competing against thirty advertising and marketing agencies across the United States. After an enormous amount of work, the competition was down to two firms: Joey's and the largest advertising agency in the world. He found out that a large group of executives from Del Taco was going to have dinner at an upscale Mexican Restaurant in Dallas, Texas, to make the final decision between the two companies. Joey decided he could not just wait by the phone for the decision. He had to do something. So while he was having margaritas at a local Mexican restaurant in Atlanta and waiting for inspiration to hit, he saw the mariachi band walking through the restaurant singing songs in Spanish. This inspired Joey to act, and he did what any other level-headed business owner would do: he hired the mariachi band from the restaurant in Atlanta and flew to Dallas with them. They then took a cab to the restaurant where the Del Taco executives were having dinner and persuaded the maitre d' at the restaurant in Dallas to swap out its own mariachi band for the one Joey had flown in from Atlanta. When the band came to the executives' table, they begin singing at the top of their lungs, "Ay, yay, yay, yay ... Hire Babbit and Reiman." They then proceeded to sing the praise of his firm for the next thirty minutes.

Joey and his band returned to Atlanta shortly after, and Joey was in his office the next day when he received a call from the chairman of the board for Del Taco. He asked Joey to look out his tenth-story window in his Atlanta office building, and Joey saw a large helicopter flying twenty yards away from his window bearing a sign that said, "Congratulations BrightHouse from Del Taco." The chairman then thanked Joey and asked him if there was anything he could do for him since he greatly appreciated all of Joey's efforts and hard work. Joey asked the chairman if he would request the helicopter pilot to fly the sign fourteen floors higher. When asked why, Joey responded, "Because that is where the office of the other firm that pitched your company is located." You will not be surprised to hear that this story has become legendary in the advertising and marketing industry.[2]

Not only was Joey creative with his pitch, he executed relevant to the inside factors. He knew his bottom line was doing what needed to be done to win the account. His strengths were his creativity and resourcefulness, but he was competing against some extremely large and experienced firms. He tirelessly prepared for this moment of truth and did everything he could to ensure it went off without a hitch, even going so far as boarding a plane to Dallas with a mariachi band. Joey had a great desire to close the deal and wanted to elicit positive emotions and reactions from Del Taco. And he did, as evidenced by how they accepted his pitch.

The Outside Factors

The outside factors in any negotiation process are those that you may not have a direct grasp on and certainly cannot control on a fundamental level, but you do have the ability to prepare for these issues. Before entering into a negotiation, hone your knowledge and understanding of them so as to minimize their overall effects on your ability to succeed.

Other People's Expectations It is vital to your success in every negotiation to manage other people's expectations early in the process. People expect what you promise and will be upset when and if you fall short. Great negotiators understand the importance of working hard to never disappoint their business partners. It is vital to have high expectations for yourself and what you can deliver but to promise only what you can deliver. It is vital to take a pass at an opportunity if you have done the due diligence and determine that the potential client's or partners' expectations are not aligned with yours. I always tell my clients the same thing: "I cannot make you any promises, but no one will work smarter and harder for you and consider your best interests better than I will." By underpromising and overperforming, I am able to manage expectations and do my job in a meaningful and effective manner.

You have to understand your clients' and opponents' expectations. Once you begin to understand them, you can work toward managing them.

The Market The market dictates the negotiation process more than almost any other factor. Having a basic understanding of the supply and demand in the marketplace will do wonders for your understanding of the negotiable pieces and help you improve how you respond to the market. When one of my catchers enters into a free agent market as one of the only catchers available who can hit well, that player has a better opportunity of signing a big contract than in a saturated market where three or four strong catchers are available.

You have to understand what else is available to the party you are trying to negotiate with. Furthermore, the market may dictate different limitations and opportunities in every negotiation. Just as a team that turns larger profits can pay players more money, a business with a larger marketing and advertising budget can sign a larger endorsement deal with one of my clients than one with a smaller budget. A basic understanding of where the market is, where it is going, and how the company you are negotiating with is positioned will give you the upper hand in the negotiation process.

Your Alternatives Whether you have alternatives is not always within your control, but the best situation for any negotiator is to have choices and to be in a position where you can truly walk away. This position creates an enormous amount of leverage and allows you to negotiate without desperation, allowing you to get what you want, not what you are offered. The only way to achieve this is to have alternatives. As the saying goes, don't put all your eggs in one basket. This can be difficult to understand at times, especially if you are a small business, but as much as possible, keep your options open. When you are entering into a negotiation, your mindset should be "deal optimistic," hoping you can come to a favorable agreement but knowing that if you cannot, you put yourself in a position to move on. When you have choices, both your demeanor and the way you present yourself change. Knowing you can walk away eliminates desperation and anxiety and promotes a more confident and focused negotiation.

Your Competition You can't control your competition's resources or angle, but by doing your best to understand what they are about, you can try to offset their angle. Understanding their angle will help you position your own points in a way that will come across as valuable and relevant. You also need to try to be aware of how they view you, what relationships they may have with the party you are both trying to negotiate with, and whether their views can influence the other party. Clarity around that is imperative so you can prepare to offset it during your discussions.

Your Potential Client's Budget and Need Gain clarity around exactly what your client has to spend on the deal. Also try to understand how he values what you are offering. How does what you offer solve a problem for him? Are there cheaper options available that would solve the same problem? Can you compete with that alternative?

And sometimes it is more about need than budget. During negotiations for a free agent baseball player or a college coach for a team that is performing poorly, it may be more important to solve a problem quickly rather than to keep costs down. Can the general manager afford another year with little success? Can the team afford another season with a less-than-stellar coach? If you provide security in a vulnerable time for the other party, budget may be less of an issue for them, a situation that gives you more control.

Market Saturation A flooded market presents a particular need. You need to find a way to set your product or what you have to offer apart from others, or you need to fall back on your relationships and make sure people want to do business with you specifically rather than everyone else out there who is offering the same thing at a similar price.

Leverage the Outside Factors Game changers understand that they cannot control all factors in a negotiation, and it makes sense to maximize their time focusing on the controllables. Nevertheless, they also know an opportunity when they see it, and if there is a way to leverage an outside factor, they jump at the opportunity.

Joey Reiman is both a master idea generator and a phenomenal negotiator. In my opinion, the primary reason he is so successful in his client pitches is not that he is fearless and not that he is fully invested in his ideas. It is not even that his ideas are groundbreaking and earth-shatteringly original. The real reason Joey succeeds as one of the best idea generators of our time is that he focuses on the controllables rather than his competition or their marketing approaches. He puts his time and effort into the inside factors that he can control. But he also has a heightened awareness of the outside factors, which he recognizes may also affect whether he gets an account and keeps alert for ways he can take advantage of things normally beyond his control.

When Joey is negotiating with and pitching to clients, he does his best to turn the outside factors into manageable controllables. When he was pitching to the Days Inn Hotel for a $10 million campaign, he was going against the biggest and most successful New York ad agencies, and he knew he had no control over them. But when he received a call from the CEO of Days Inn Hotel scheduling an appointment in Atlanta with him, he was confident he would get the account, even though his firm was a David among Goliaths. When the CEO showed up, he told Joey he wanted to give the account to another firm, but would love to pay Joey for a single idea that he had previously pitched to the CEO. After thinking about it at length, Joey told the CEO that if he wanted the idea, it would come only with the account. Joey could have taken a nice payday to the bank for his single idea, but he wanted the account. He also knew that his potential client loved his idea and Joey believed he could leverage that to close the deal.

Once Joey realized that the client's motivation to acquire the idea was high, it made sense to offer a take-it-or-leave-it package. Joey also knew his client had the budget to spend and it was going to go somewhere, so he decided to take his great idea and use it as a catalyst to negotiate an even better deal, turning a potentially small payday into a $10 million account.[3] You control a potential's partner's motivation and budget, but by understanding these things clearly, taking a bold step, and offering an ultimatum, Joey leveraged those outside factors to his advantage, which resulted in a huge win.

When it comes to any negotiation, it is not enough to just be aware of these outside factors, although that is a start. The most successful negotiators take what would initially seem to be an uncontrollable factor and mold them into something they can guide, direct, and use to strengthen their own position.

Negotiating Like the Best

The best have a unique and insightful understanding of how to optimize the negotiation process and obtain what they value and desire, all while leaving their business partners feeling satisfied and content. One of the fundamental characteristics that the best carry throughout negotiating is they always consider their business counterparts. In any negotiation, if the other side is unhappy, no "good" deal will be done. The best understand this concept and work hard to make sure that after the deal is done, the parties aren't angry or bitter about the outcome, but rather that everyone walks away happy and with what they negotiated.

In good negotiations, there are no winners and losers. The most important thing in any negotiation is getting a great outcome. Using terms like *winning* and *losing* implies that you are in combat. There is an art to negotiation, and when it is over, all negotiations are measured by how pleased you are, your company is, and your counterpart or client may be. Great deals result in mutual benefit and reciprocal happiness. If you are thrilled and your client is unhappy, have you really succeeded in your negotiations? If you are thrilled but you have severely burned a bridge, was the negotiation a success? So instead of discussing how to win when negotiating, let's look at what the best do to optimize every negotiation.

Every negotiation I am a part of is a learning process. Throughout the years, I have truly found a happy medium between getting a great deal for my clients and creating a situation where the other side feels that they have walked away in a better position as well. If you rob the other side blind in a negotiation, they will recognize this and may try to avoid doing business with you in the future. The business of being an agent is no different from any other business in that relationships matter as much as or more than the outcome of the deal.

The Deal Is in the Details

In the negotiation process, the sum of the parts is always greater than the whole. The best understand that the difference between getting the deal and losing it is in a few small details. These details add up over the course of a negotiation and create a tipping point of sorts. When all the pieces are in place, the negotiation is going well, but when one small thing goes wrong or isn't addressed properly, the whole thing falls apart. If you focus on the details of the negotiation, all of that attention will add up to the consummation of a deal.

Let's look at the details you should consider throughout the negotiation process in order to close the deal of your life. This list represents only some of the things you will need to consider; each negotiation will have a unique set of circumstances and a unique set of details you must pay attention to.

Dress the Part

How you are perceived is important. So dressing the part should be obvious, but amazingly, it is not for many people. Always consider your audience, and dress appropriately. A suit may not always be right for your pitch. If you are meeting with clients who are laid back and casual, it can be to your benefit to consider jeans and a button-down shirt, for example. Dressing the part requires considering what the part may actually be. I call it the mirror effect. When you walk in the door to begin negotiating, the other side should see themselves in the way you dress, the way you present yourself, and certainly the way you interact.

For example, if you are meeting with a client who works for a large corporation, you should consider dressing more professionally in a suit or at least business casual attire. However, if your potential client or the individual with whom you are negotiating is more casual, consider dressing down in order to mirror the other side's style. When you think about how to dress for a negotiation, consider the age, background, and type of work your potential client does, and factor that into your decision on what to wear.

Insight Is Income

You have to clearly understand the other side's needs and desires. Before you go into the negotiation, acquire this valuable knowledge. But during the negotiation, there is also a wealth of information that you can acquire from the other side that will help your position. The best way to acquire it is by asking questions. When I negotiate, I ask question after question: open ended, leading, long, short, theoretical, and realistic. In a sense, you are cross-examining them, and if you are good at this, they may not realize what you are doing.

When negotiating, always consider asking the who, what, where, when, and why questions. After leaving the negotiation table, you should have at least a basic understanding of who your client is, what this person wants to achieve by negotiating, and where his or her basic need may be. When does the client need to close the deal? And why will the client choose your option over other people in a similar position?

From coaching my clients on how to deal with the media, I have learned that great reporters ask a question and then listen. They are quiet, do not interrupt, and allow the other side to answer the questions fully and completely. That is what you

I always say that insight is income.

want to do during negotiations. I want the other side to talk and disclose more information so I better know how to make use of it. The more they offer, the more I know. I always say that insight is income.

Listen

Asking without listening is just as bad as not asking at all. And sometimes it is even worse if the other side does not sense you are engaged in what they have to say. When you truly listen, you block everything else out and imagine that nothing matters but the next word out of that person's mouth. Focus on the person you are speaking to, and gather data.

Processing and understanding the information you are receiving will give you priceless insight. Listen for the person's tone, timing, and message. Is she getting loud? Does her tone of voice seem anxious or nervous? Does she present her facts in a confident or an insecure way? Does she talk about a situation in a way that gives you a sense that she has choices? Active listening skills are important to successful negotiation.

Throw in Some Zingers

I call these healthy jabs. They are unexpected, challenging, and often aggressive statements that point out the strength of your position and are especially useful if you want to gauge the other side's reaction to something. Once when I was negotiating with a team, I turned to the general manager and said, "Look. It is no mystery that your team was dead last in the MLB in home runs. You guys need some power." I could quickly tell I made him generally uncomfortable, but it was also self-serving, pointing out the 800-pound gorilla in the room while demonstrating how giving my guy a deal would help him score runs. Zingers are not ill-willed or malicious. They are intended to remind the other side of the quick facts in a slightly heightened aggressive tone.

Not all zingers are good ones. You want to play to the other side's emotions without making that person feel too uncomfortable. People negotiate to fulfill a need, so I find it important to always hit on those needs with my comments. My advice is to push the line but not overstep it. For example, my statement regarding home runs was a good jab. A bad zinger would have been, "It is no mystery you were dead last in the MLB in home runs because your hitting coach doesn't have a clue and you keep signing bad talent." That zinger could upset the other side and put him or her on the defensive. Healthy jabs lead to constructive results, but be savvy and careful when you push the line.

Insert Levity

The stakes can be enormously high in a negotiation: jobs may be at risk, businesses and millions of dollars may be in the balance, and egos and feelings can certainly be hurt. Insert some humor into the situation when appropriate, and keep it light. I always try to create a casual and natural atmosphere so the other side is comfortable. If the people you are negotiating with feel that they can speak freely and openly while discussing their concerns and desires, they will be more likely to work with you instead of against you.

Focus on Body Language

During negotiations, body language says a lot. Body language, in fact, is just as important as verbal statements, and maybe more so because it is difficult to mask and manipulate your body language. You may be hearing no, but the body language is clearly telling you yes. It is vital to compare nonverbal cues to verbal ones. If they match, you know you are in the clear, but when you are seeing mixed signals and disconnect, you have to question the other side.

Warren Steed Jeffs, one of the FBI's ten most wanted fugitives as the head of a religious cult that arranged marriages between adult males and underage girls, was riding in the back seat of his friend's car in 2006 when a Las Vegas trooper pulled the car over for an improper license plate. During his investigation, the trooper noticed Jeffs in the back seat, eating a salad, and refusing to make eye contact with the trooper. The trooper also noticed that the man's carotid artery, the large neck vein, was thumping up and down. This body language caused concern for the trooper. Although Jeffs answered his questions with words that should normally not garner alarm, the trooper saw these contravening nonverbal cues. After a quick diagnosis, he arrested Jeffs and quickly discovered he had just taken one of the top ten most-wanted people off of the streets, and all because he interpreted the dangerous man's body language.[4]

Focusing on body language in a negotiation or any other situation may tip you on the other side's emotions, feelings, or temperament. They may always tell you they are giving you their best offer, but if you read their body language accurately, it may prevent you and your client from leaving money on the table.

Connect with Their Bottom Line

Another important detail to focus on when negotiating is how you can connect with your potential business partner's bottom line. In any negotiation, it is important to demonstrate to the person on the other side of the table how you can fill his pockets. I work hard to do this in creative ways, some of which the other party may have not even considered. In any negotiation, come prepared with one or two facts that illustrate that you have fully considered how this deal will benefit the other side and that are clearly creative and connect to their bottom line. For example, if am discussing the impact a player may have on a baseball team, I can pull gate attendance numbers and say something like, "When he pitches, there are an extra twenty thousand people in attendance." Or I can pull sales of jerseys with my player's name on them and compare them with those of other players in the Major Leagues. My client may sell more jerseys than anyone else on the team. When you demonstrate that you understand and can contribute to the bottom line, you are building trust and leveling the playing field, allowing you to build on that foundation.

Validate Your Arguments

Always support your arguments with valid facts. This seems obvious, but one unsupported or undocumented claim can change the scope of the deal. When you tell the other side that your firm can take him places that others cannot, you have to justify this statement with data or examples because his next question will be, "How?"

If you are trying to increase sales, make sure you know what sales numbers were over the past several years. Demonstrate by using hard facts how you can increase net revenue. All baseball contracts and statistics are public information; they are easy to validate and even easier to negate. Nevertheless, I always know my players' statistics. On the flip side, golf contracts are not public information, but if you are dealing with a company that does contracts with numerous golfers, sales reps there will have an idea when your data are valid and when they are inflated. Don't round up, don't move a decimal, and don't deal in generalities. Be precise, be consistent, and definitely be accurate.

Join Them for Coffee

I always joke that you can tell if someone really likes you if she will sit down and have a cup of coffee with you before, after, or during the process. Our world is competitive, and relationships, more than anything else, win out. When all the numbers are the same, the company will do business with people its leaders like over people they don't like.

Mold Problems into Solutions

When you are negotiating, remember that you are attempting to offer someone a solution to a problem. The people you are negotiating with you see you as someone who will bring them solutions. Let's say they need strong sales leadership. No problem, you say; here is how you can provide that. They need a reorganization of their brand. Okay, you say, you can handle it. Always anticipate problems that may come between you and the deal, and prepare for them. This is one part strategic, one part problem solving, and one part what I like to call 360-degree awareness, which means you are aware of everything that is going on in the negotiation. If you have these three characteristics, you will be well positioned to take the other side's hurdles and turn them into stepping-stones.

Anthony J. D'Angelo, a writer and thinker, once said, "Focus 90% of your time on solutions and only 10% of your time on problems."[5] That is how you should handle negotiations. Acknowledge there could be a potential hurdle to closing the deal, and spend your time focusing on how you are going to blow through this obstacle.

People appreciate solutions, and they value preparation. If you enter the negotiation room having already identified any problems and sculpted a viable solution that benefits both parties, the deal is yours to lose.

Turn Defensiveness into Curiosity

In negotiations, curiosity helps close the deal. It is vital to any negotiation to always show interest in your potential business partner and avoid defensive behaviors. Curiosity accomplishes two separate and distinct goals. First, it shows that you are truly engaged and dedicated to communicating and finding out the most valuable information about your business partner's ideals and desires. Second, it offers an avenue to gain insight and information.

It is important to press the other side for information but never react negatively or defensively to their responses. Defensiveness shows insecurity, as if you are putting up a wall. You are also more inclined to speak with your heart and not your head. Instead of bracing yourself and picking a fight or leaving the situation altogether, go into curiosity mode. Do this by asking questions. Instead of defending, inquire. When someone I'm negotiating with tells me that he doesn't see value in my client, I don't get angry, and I certainly don't say, "You have to be kidding me! How do you think people win? They drive in runs!" Rather, I respond, "So it sounds like you're saying that it's not just RBIs [runs batted in] that win ball games. Is that right? What do you value?" Remain composed, calculated, and coherent, never falling victim to your emotions or reacting in a way that cuts the negotiation short. Remember, insight equals income.

Find Different Ways to Negotiate the Same Outcome

William Ury, a mediator, writer, and speaker who focuses on conflict resolution, told a story from the Middle East about three brothers whose father left them seventeen camels. He left one brother half of these camels, one brother a third of these camels, and the other brother one-ninth of these camels. Well, since two, three, and nine do not go into seventeen, brotherly patience ran out. Thus, the brothers went to a wise woman and asked her for help with their problem. She thought long and hard and came back and said that although she did not have a solution, she did have a camel that she could give them. They now had eighteen camels: one brother took nine camels, the other took six camels, and the last one took two camels. They now had one camel left, and they thanked the old wise woman and gave her back her camel.[6]

This story epitomizes the way I view negotiation. When it comes to negotiating, what is important is the outcome, not necessarily how you get there. My goal is to get to a mutually beneficial resolution with honesty and dignity. One tactic I often use to ensure I get the best deal is to give the other side a few options to get to the resolution (or number) that I am presenting as fair. Offering the other side multiple options in the negotiation process is highly effective. Most people have a sticking point in negotiations, that is, the number or issue on which they won't budge from. For most of my clients, this is usually the base salary or guaranteed money. Most deals are lost in the meat of the negotiation, not the details, so to close the deal, I always consider alternative strategies to get to the same figure.

When I was negotiating an endorsement deal for Matt Kuchar, a successful PGA Tour golfer, we had a potential endorsement deal from a huge company, but we disagreed on his base salary. Instead of trying to negotiate on the base salary, which appeared to be the other side's sticking point, we focused our negotiations on the incentive bonuses and the escalating clauses. Although they did not budge on the base retainer, we negotiated some lucrative incentives for Matt that we believed were surely attainable. We were confident he would hit many of these goals and that they would make up the difference in the base plus some. We were right, and Matt made more money with his incentive-laden contract than he would have with a larger base. We all bet on each other, and while it may have been a riskier move for us on the front end, Matt was confident in his ability to deliver and it was the best track to secure the best possible result.

Remember that there are lots of ways to get to the same destination, so always plot numerous ways to get to the same outcome. You never know which one will end up getting you there.

Timing Is of the Essence

Timing can be the difference between closing the deal and losing it. It all starts with being aware of the things that are happening around you. If the company you are negotiating with just reported poor earnings or lost a large piece of business, then the last thing you want to do is ask them for a large chunk of money. If that company has just received bad press, explain to them how you can help clean this up and bring them something positive to talk about. You have to understand what the other side is experiencing. Bad circumstances for the other side may or may not be great timing for you; it depends on the specifics of the situation. Good timing, along with an understanding of when you should act and when you should react, will help your position in the constant back-and-forth of negotiation.

When Negotiations Go Wrong

The smallest misstep or mistake can cause a seemingly rock-solid deal to fall apart. One unnecessary statement or small deviation from the agreed-on terms can cause irreparable damage to an otherwise strong relationship. It's true that you should always approach a negotiation as if you know you will succeed, but be confident, not cocky. Even when you are prepared, sometimes negotiations don't go according to plan. However, that does not mean you need to lose the deal. When things begin to go wrong, think about these skills and techniques that some of the best negotiators in the world use to save deals.

Retreat and Revisit

Everyone has bad days from time to time, and there will be instances when you and the person you are negotiating with will be unable to connect for a myriad reasons not necessarily directly related to the deal. Or there may be some other reason that things are not aligning for your deal. Whatever the reason, it is okay. There is no reason to keep going. It is perfectly acceptable, when you face this kind of a difficult situation, to agree to pause and revisit it later.

In numerous negotiations, I have been able to tell that things were not going well and that nothing was going to change that at that moment, so I acknowledged the lack of progress and asked if we could schedule a time to reconnect. After a few days, we revisited the issue, and many times, this interlude made an enormous difference.

Don't be afraid to leave the negotiation table and come back when everyone has had a chance to relax. Sometimes that break can change everyone's attitude and feelings.

Take Baby Steps

I always tell my clients that negotiating is about hitting singles, not home runs. Often it's easier to get a little here and a little there rather than trying to get everything at once. It will be crystal clear if you push too far (and it will be clear to you when this happens), you have to refocus and take baby steps. When you try to get it all at once, you seem eager and even pushy to the other side.

A negotiation is rarely completed in one meeting. Most of my deals extend over the course of days, weeks, and sometimes months. Watch the small victories tally up. Get a little here and a little there over the duration of the negotiation, and you will find that you have gotten more than you would have if you went for it all at once.

When in Doubt, Apologize

We all misspeak sometimes. When it happens, apologize rather than walk away or deny the misstatement. Acknowledging it with an apology can quickly change the way everyone perceives the situation. Demonstrating to the other side that you are humble, accountable, and willing to take responsibility for your words and deeds means a lot. Even if you are not totally in the wrong, sometimes acknowledging the difficulty of a situation can be a healthy way to work toward a resolution. Put your ego aside, and focus on your goals.

> *If an apology can change the temperature of the negotiation, offer it freely and voluntarily.*

If an apology can change the temperature of the negotiation, offer it freely and voluntarily. Be creative when apologizing. Don't just call and say, "I'm sorry." Demonstrate it with sincere actions—perhaps send a small token by way of apology, or a hand-written card, or lunch for the firm. Do something that shows that you care enough to put effort into your apology.

Change the Subject

When things are heating up, for good or for bad, I sometimes shift gears. One of my favorite negotiation tools is changing the subject. It does two primary things: establishes control and provides you with time to think. Negotiations can occur at the speed of light, and a few moments to reflect and think about your answer can make a significant difference in the flow of the negotiation.

Like anything else in life, negotiations have their ups and downs. You can't win them all, but if you work hard and focus your attention on the game changers, you will perfect your skill set and become a force to be reckoned with. When you think you have lost the deal, consider the ways you can regain control of the situation. Use these techniques to redirect the momentum in a way that is beneficial to you, and you will have the potential to excel in every negotiation.

Head, Shoulders, Knees, and Toes

It takes a lot to truly become a master negotiator. Time, effort, understanding, preparation, knowledge, communication, intelligence, discipline, vision, desire, and character build a track record and are just a few of the skills all great negotiators understand. Remembering of all these things and drawing on all of the techniques and information regarding negotiations can be difficult in the heat of the moment.

With that in mind I've simplified things a bit. Whenever you are negotiating, if you remember nothing else, consider the childhood song, "Head, Shoulders, Knees, and Toes":

Head. Use your head. You have to trust your instincts and think quickly. You have worked hard to train yourself to handle the negotiation process, so don't fall short. You know what you are doing, and you understand where your bottom line is; think clearly and use your knowledge and common sense. And always tell the truth so you don't have to waste time trying to remember what you said.

Shoulders. Shoulder the burden of preparing for the negotiation process. Take on the responsibility, and make sure that when you enter the negotiation room, there are no unexpected hurdles that will come between you and the deal.

Knees. Don't let your knees shake. Stay focused, and do not let emotions, nerves, or anxiety get the best of you. If you are properly prepared, you have nothing to worry about. Don't let threats or the fear of losing the deal push you into a bad decision or even one that leaves you uncomfortable. Stand strong, and don't let anyone see you waver.

Toes. Your toes may be some of the smallest bones in your body, but without them, you cannot stand on your own two feet. The same is true with the details in any negotiation. The details are what make the difference between a good deal and a great deal. Negotiate the bottom line, but remember that learning how to handle the small parts of the negotiation process will differentiate you from the competition and propel you into the realm of the elite.

Negotiation is a lifeline for businesses and individuals. It offers parties a medium to communicate, expand, grow, and come together to form strong relationships that improve their businesses and their products. Becoming a successful negotiator takes time, effort, and a dedication to staying in it and working through all the difficulties that will arise. But the end is a worthwhile goal, and hard work creates measurable results. Negotiation is a skill that can be both learned and developed, and by learning from the best and educating yourself about the techniques and skills that the best implement in their negotiations, you will be well on your way to becoming the best negotiator you can be.

3

Communicate Your Way to Success

Communication works for those that work at it.
—John Powell

Communication is an important skill to understand and a powerful tool to master. Great communicators understand that the goal of communication is twofold: to share ideas for personal and professional development and to form relationships. The best are diligent and passionate about doing both. There are almost limitless ways to communicate verbally and nonverbally. We communicate with our voice, body language, tone, attitude, expressions, silence, timing, and appearance, to name just a few. But with so many different ways to communicate, it can be difficult to know which way is the best. And since we use different mediums at the same time when communicating, sometimes choosing the best combination of those mediums is just as important. The best are adept at choosing the most effective method of communication for a given situation, and they understand that the situation itself often dictates how to communicate. They also know that often it is not even what you choose to communicate but rather how you communicate that makes the difference.

The best use communication as a powerful way to achieve success, and they work constantly to improve their ability to reach great peaks through communicating. This chapter focuses on how to maximize the communicative process and use it as a tool to promote better business and better relationships.

Sharing Ideas

One of the most important aspects of communication is how we share ideas. Sharing ideas with someone else can broaden the way both parties look at the world and can change the way both think about success and how to achieve it. It can offer new opportunities and lead to a rethinking of old ways of doing things. When we share ideas, we offer one another the chance for change and the opportunity to increase our potential in business and in the rest of life.

Communicating Creatively

When you are communicating, it is important not only to get your message across, but to do so with maximum impact. Communicating creatively is a skill that is vital to your success because it will set you apart from the competition. It's one thing to deliver a message. It's another thing entirely to do so in a way that is unforgettable in the most positive sense of the word.

When Joey Reiman and his ideation firm, BrightHouse, designed a pitch for Cadillac, Joey invited the model's top executives to his Atlanta-based office. They were intrigued with Joey's firm, but they were concerned that his company did not understand their cars.

When the executives arrived at Joey's firm, they were escorted into the conference room—and found a full-sized Cadillac sedan in the middle of it. They were astounded and curious, because there was no way the car could have been transported into the conference room on the tenth floor of an office building in the middle of a major city. After a few minutes, Joey informed them that he knew they were concerned that the people at BrightHouse didn't have enough knowledge of cars, so they decided to take one apart. His company had taken the car apart and brought it to the office in pieces, where they reassembled it.

Joey won the account. Communicating creatively to Cadillac that he would go the extra mile to understand the ins and outs of how their cars were made was a game changer.[1] Joey's goal in this pitch was to share a unique idea and communicate to his potential client that he knew Cadillac cars. He came up with a bold way to do just that.

Joey's story demonstrates the power of innovative communication. If you know your goal and dig into the heart of it, you can better identify exactly what you want to communicate. You also will be able to work hard to present that goal and share that idea in the best and most creative way imaginable.

All communication starts with sharing an idea, a basic concept that you must never overlook. It is the backbone of the communication process. The idea that Joey was trying to share with the people at Cadillac was that he and his team understood, and went to extremes to learn about, the ins and outs of cars, and he found a truly creative and effective way to communicate exactly that.

Sharing Ideas to Fix Problems

When Arthur Blank bought the Atlanta Falcons, the club was having trouble selling out games, so Arthur began taking steps to reduce the empty seats in the stadium. The first thing he did was at a grassroots level: reach out to the general public and ask them why they were not buying tickets to the games. Arthur wanted the general public to share with him their reservations about purchasing tickets and any ideas about what he could change to encourage them to purchase. He found there were only a few substantial and consistent reasons that people weren't buying tickets, including the team's overall performance and the experience fans had when attending the games, so he went to work to gain clarity from the source relevant to each of the issues.

Through reaching out to the consumers, Arthur saved endless time and money guessing at ways to fix the problem, and he quickly achieved his desired result: as of the 2010 season, the Atlanta Falcons were selling out every game and won over 90 percent of their home games in the 2009 and 2010 seasons.[2]

Sharing Ideas to Create Business

Tony Conway, CEO and founder of A Legendary Event, always says to his employees, "We don't wait for the phone to ring. We make the phone ring." Tony has a policy at his company that the best way to create business is to reach out. His employees tirelessly share ideas with clients. They often call their clients with ideas for events and parties for the upcoming moments in their lives. It is not uncommon for Tony's clients to receive calls months before their birthday, holidays, or anniversaries with ideas about how they can celebrate those special events.[3]

Through communicating and sharing ideas, Tony strategically builds his business from the inside out. He reaches out to his customers and makes sure their phones ring. He believes that this is a practical, powerful, and pragmatic approach, and he has built his business through these phone calls and his genuine concern for customers. By sharing ideas with his customers, he infuses energy into his business and keeps people connected with his brand.

Communicating for Success

These three stories are examples of how the best businesspeople think. Good businesspeople communicate; but great businesspeople share ideas. Whether it was Joey sharing his vision for a car company by communicating creatively, or Arthur fixing the problems with his team by asking the general public to share their concerns with him, or Tony reaching out to his customers and sharing ideas that might appeal to them and bring him business at the same time, each of these businessmen understands the power of sharing ideas and has used it to build business and improve operation. If you want to be extraordinarily successful in business, you have to look at communication as a way to share ideas.

Good businesspeople communicate; but great businesspeople share ideas.

Forming Relationships

Sharing ideas creates a powerful platform to form relationships as well. In this way, you build business contacts and friendships and create networking opportunities, referral sources, and resources. The greatest communicators focus just as much time and energy on connecting with people and forming and strengthening relationships while communicating as they do sharing ideas. During the communication process, connecting with people should be one of your main goals. People do business with those whom they relate to and those they like. Forming relationships outside the negotiation process will help you increase your success inside the negotiation process.

Ernie Johnson Jr. is a highly successful broadcaster, sports commentator, and analyst. He works with former National Basketball Association greats Charles Barkley and Kenny Smith on TNT doing the pregame, halftime, and postgame shows for network coverage of the games. And he is also an announcer for Major League Baseball on TBS and the PGA Championship.

During his first PGA Tour broadcast, Ernie was a little nervous, so before he went on air, he approached Verne Lundquist, a veteran golf announcer and recent inductee into the National Sportscasters and Sportswriters Association's Hall of Fame. Verne had been covering PGA events for years, and Ernie asked him to share any ideas, advice, or guidance he might have before the two went on air. Verne took the time to sit down with Ernie and gave him some hints and tips about how he could perform well. Verne was encouraging and not only shared some pointers with Ernie but also formed a relationship with him during that time.[4] By forming a relationship with Verne before going on air for the first time, Ernie was at ease and comfortable, and he was able to perform at a higher level and succeed in an otherwise stressful and high-anxiety situation. The simple task of communicating with Verne created a level of insight and ease that he otherwise would not have had.

In this situation, Verne demonstrated the pillars of communication: sharing and forming relationships. The two have remained friends throughout the years, and Ernie gained a valuable mentor he can turn to when he needs professional guidance. And it all started with Ernie's willingness to be vulnerable and Verne's willingness to take the time to connect.

Sharing ideas with the intent to connect accelerates and motivates the formation of relationships. From the best communicators, we learn that if we focus communication on connecting in hopes of forming a relationship, we will take something greater than just information from the process.

Most people communicate for information: they want an answer or need direction. But if you reshape your goals and focus on connecting and forming relationships, you will get the most from communicating with others.

What Great Communicators Know

While all great communicators understand the importance of sharing ideas and forming relationships, the difference between being a great communicator and being the best is the understanding that the communicative process is a subtle art. It is not only about taking the time to communicate, but approaching communication in a way that is respectful and engaging, and puts the person you are communicating with at ease.

This section focuses on how go-getters and game changers go about sharing ideas and forming relationships. These are intricate skills, and incorporating them into your communicative repertoire will enable you to become a more effective and successful communicator.

Communication Must Be Based on Mutual Respect

The best communicators know that communication takes work. Sharing ideas and forming relationships not only requires you to understand the people you are communicating with but also to respect and place value on them.

Bob Burg is a business speaker and *Wall Street Journal* best-selling coauthor of *The Go-Giver: A Little Story About a Powerful Business Idea*.[5] The premise is that shifting focus from getting to giving (meaning constantly and consistently adding value to people's lives) is not only a good way to live life but a profitable way. Bob believes that when it comes to communication, the best win without intimidation. They focus on how to get what they want while making others feel good about themselves, and they are able to communicate in a way to bring out their own best while accomplishing what they want to.[6]

Great communicators understand Bob's lesson about respecting one another during the communication process. In this approach to communicating, you not only recognize the value in the process itself, but you also recognize that the other person is a valuable part of that process. If you respect both the process and the person, you will find that you can move mountains while communicating. You have to communicate in a conscious manner, with honor and integrity; otherwise people will not want communicate with or do business with you. If you don't have respect for them, they certainly won't want to share ideas with you or form a relationship with you.

Sometimes Less Is More

Sometimes what we don't say is just as important as what we do say. The truly best communicators have a situational understanding of when to actively participate in the communication process and when to take a step back. Sometimes a simple yes or no is enough to communicate an answer. Other situations may require an explanation or an engaging discussion. Whatever the case may be, be certain that you are aware of the situation and how the other person is feeling.

More often than not, the situation will dictate how and how much you should communicate. You also need to be aware of yourself and your tendencies and patterns. If you are prone to talking a lot and dominating conversations, be sure to keep yourself in check. You never want to be remembered or have a reputation for producing an uninteresting monologue. And in fact, sometimes two or three sharp and focused words can take the place of hundreds of blurred and unfocused sentences. I have learned from the best communicators that sometimes the message is not in how much you say, but rather how effective the words you choose to say are.

Sometimes the message is not in how much you say, but rather how effective the words you choose to say are.

Joey Reiman, like all other great communicators, understands that sometimes less is more. Once when he was pitching an antismoking campaign to the American Cancer Society, he hired a billboard company to put up an uncomfortably large and towering billboard over a cemetery with the words "Smoking Section" in large writing. This bold move landed Joey the account. Two simple words on a powerful visual backdrop communicated a riveting message to onlookers. And in this situation, less truly was more.

It can take very little to share a compelling message if you focus your thoughts on quality rather than quantity. It is not about how much, but rather how powerful, your message is.[7]

Words Have Power

Words change relationships and lives. If you don't think so, consider a time in your life when someone said something to you that has stuck with you to this day. If you can remember such a time, then the words that he or she chose or the lesson you learned from this exchange has quite likely made a profound difference in the person you have become. That is proof enough that words have meaning and power. It is up to you how you choose to use them.

The best recognize the power of words and use it to their advantage. They focus on word choice and recognize the opportunity that language presents. When the best communicate, they are resoundingly efficient in achieving their goals. They choose their words carefully and deliver them with ease and flow, because they understand the significance behind those choices.

Rarely do we realize the power of our words until we say something that results in a negative outcome. We know it as the old "foot-in-the-mouth" adage. But what about the power of positive words? When someone is not feeling well, tell that person you hope he or she feels better. When someone is supportive, thank that person. When someone is having a bad day, ask if you can help. These kinds of positive words go a long way to creating and strengthening relationships.

Ernie Johnson Jr. is a cancer survivor. He was diagnosed with non-Hodgkin's lymphoma and had a public battle with cancer, which he won. The most reassuring and comforting support he had were the e-mails, letters, and phone calls from people wishing him well and offering encouragement during this tough time in his life. He believes that those words were powerful and that "people just have to click Send."

Ernie was referring to the idea that people sometimes sit down to type an e-mail or offer the support of words, but don't follow through. Or they may think something but not say it. I am willing to bet that the reason people do not click Send is that they do not understand or believe in the power of words. Words are powerful, and Ernie, who fully recovered from his bout with cancer, will tell you that those who clicked Send made all of the difference in his recovery. The spirit and motivation these letters and e-mails infused into his battle helped Ernie to build the strength he needed to fight and beat cancer.[8]

William Arthur Ward, a twentieth-century author and teacher known for his inspirational words, said, "Feeling gratitude and not expressing it is like wrapping a present and not giving it." You have to put yourself out there and communicate. Don't just think about communicating. Do it. You thought about something for a reason, and if it can have a positive impact on someone else, then say it. More often than not, people know that their actions will make a difference, yet they still choose not to act.

If you can make a positive difference, then do so. The power of words is enormous. Use them wisely, well, and willingly.

Be Interested, Not Interesting

It is better to be interested than interesting. One of the most important characteristics of a good communicator is to ask questions and listen to and think about the responses. The best communicators are the greatest listeners, not necessarily the greatest talkers.

Scott Lindy is a program director for Star 94, an Atlanta-based top-40-hits radio station. When he was hired, he asked the station to change his job title from "program director" to "listener advocate." He saw the goal of his job as increasing and maintaining an audience and therefore should be reflected in his job title. The station happily agreed.

Scott once had an eye-opening and inspirational meeting with one of the world's most skilled communicators, Bill Clinton, president at that time. When Scott met Bill Clinton, he was conflicted. A Republican, Scott was a bit wary and reluctant to open up. But when he approached the president, Clinton grabbed Scott's hand with both of his and began asking him questions about what he did for a living. When Clinton discovered that Scott was working for a successful country music station, he preceded to quiz Scott on country music, maintaining eye contact the entire time, and telling Scott what he liked about that music. Clinton was fully engaged in the conversation and showed enormous interest in Scott and his career and interests. Jokingly, Scott says he considers President Clinton a close friend. While Scott may be joking about their relationship, there is much truth and validity to his feelings. Clinton had shown him that that conversation was his top priority at that moment. Clinton took five minutes out of his fully booked schedule, engaged his mind and senses, and focused on Scott Lindy as if he was the only person in the world that mattered at that time.[9]

The best communicators know that if you engage another person and really focus on being interested in what that person is saying, you will also be engaging in one of the fundamentals of communication: forming relationships.

Bill Clinton is a master communicator. He is interested in and warm toward the people with whom he is communicating. He is focused. He has held what many consider to be the most powerful position in the world. Yet when he communicates, it is not about him but about the other person and that person's interests. Take a lesson from the former president, and be interested, not interesting; engaged, not engaging; and focused, not focusing on something else. These are things that all successful communicators know and take to heart.

Say What You Mean, and Mean What You Say

Whenever you communicate, you must be true to your word and communicate with honor. You have to be consistent, and your actions have to support your promises. I see people often overextend themselves and overpromise when communicating. The best generally have complex and busy schedules, so it easy for them to commit to things that they cannot actually execute. Nevertheless, the most successful communicators understand the importance of setting boundaries and managing expectations they can meet and honoring the other person with solid guarantees. It is much easier to say "no" in the beginning than "I am sorry" later. If you create realistic expectations from the start, you will be less likely to let people down.

The best communicators understand that there is a significant difference between saying what you mean and meaning what you say. Saying what you mean is about communicating directly; meaning what you say is about doing it authentically. When you say what you mean, you are communicating to those on the other side in a direct manner. You tell them what you are feeling, give them any information they are asking for, and don't conceal anything. People appreciate this because you are demonstrating that you value their time, respect their integrity, and value their intelligence. No one wants to feel that someone is dancing around the issue or not being absolutely truthful. When you hide things or talk in circles, others will assume that you are not saying what you mean and therefore are not genuine or honest. When you mean what you say, you are making the other side a promise. Whatever comes out of your mouth will be the end result. People are responsive and grateful for reliability and consistency. When you mean what you say, you are establishing these steadfast principles.

Saying what you mean is about communicating directly; meaning what you say is about doing it authentically.

In the business world, long-term success is often dependent on your reputation. People want to do business with those who communicate authentically and then deliver, not just those who communicate. When I tell my players I will do something, I do it. I deliver. Because if I don't, I know that they won't value my word.

Tony Conway says that "when it comes to our customers, we make them a promise. We put that promise in writing and ensure we keep it. Unlike most businesses, our customers cannot take our product off the rack and try it on. The end result is the end result, so all we can do before the big event is keep the promise to put on a spectacular event."[10] Tony and his company are the epitome of the phrase, "Say what you mean, and mean what you say."

When communicating, remember to say both what you mean and mean what you say. Be direct, and execute your promises. These are two simple and fundamental beliefs that the best know are pillars of the communicative process.

Be Open to Other Opinions

The process of communication is fluid, and your opinions within that process should be as well. When it comes to communication, never hold on to your opinions so tightly that you aren't open to new information or don't listen to what others are saying. Sometimes you are right, but other times not so much. You should always be willing to listen to and think about what other people are saying. Everyone has biases and leanings, and the best in our society have firm convictions and are steadfast in their beliefs. But they also are willing to change their views and modify their opinions in the face of new and compelling information. This goes back to the idea of turning defensiveness into curiosity. If you are defensive about or unwavering in your opinions, you will brush people to the side and create a challenging obstacle to reaching one of the goals of the communication process: forming relationships.

You need to adjust your opinions if there are significant reasons to do so. Welcome change and the chance to reshape your feelings and thinking in light of new information. It really comes down to listening with an open mind to what people are saying.

Nelson Mandela once said, "As a leader . . . I have always endeavored to listen to what each and every person in a discussion had to say before venturing my own opinion. Oftentimes, my own opinion will simply represent a consensus of what I heard in the discussion. I always remember the axiom: a leader is like a shepherd. He stays behind the flock, letting the most nimble go out ahead, whereupon the others follow, not realizing that all along they are being directed from behind."[11] Mandela truly breathes life into the concept that flexibility in communicating opinions is vital to forming a comfortable and beneficial relationship with others.

None of us enjoy being told we are wrong; what we want is to be heard and listened to. If you allow your predispositions and opinions to lead your communicative behavior, they will act like a shield, deflecting opportunities and potential relationships before they have the chance to reach you.

Make the Other Person Feel Safe

It is important to create a comfortable backdrop for the communication process where you welcome both the people and their opinions. People will close themselves off and be unwilling to offer information if you don't create a safe environment for them to do so. If you do not make people feel safe, you are losing an opportunity to connect.

When communicating, create an atmosphere that will make those on the other side willing to open up to you. They have to feel comfortable and safe that their opinions and feelings will be welcomed rather than attacked. First and foremost when working to make people feel safe, you have to relate to them. This means you need to be interested, not interesting, and that starts with asking questions and being a good listener. Next, you have to be passive, not aggressive. Welcome differing opinions, and never attack the person. It is okay to disagree, but do so in a respectful manner and always explain why you are disagreeing. Insight will create acceptance. If those on the other side know why you differ in your opinion, they will feel safe and comfortable enough to engage in dialogue. Finally, you have to let the other parties know they are heard by simply reflecting back to them what you heard them say.

Thoughts are reflections of people's innermost feelings and beliefs. Therefore, they are windows into who people really are and how they feel about something. They share their thoughts in the hope that others will accept those thoughts. If they feel comfortable and believe their thoughts will be accepted, those thoughts will be more insightful and value driven. When you make people safe, they open up their innermost thoughts to you. Every person has an inner lockbox where they keep their most important thoughts and secrets. Your job is to make people feel comfortable enough to give you the key to the lockbox so that you can gain insight into what they think, how they feel, and what is important to them, thereby forging a closer connection.

The communication process should be a breeding ground for ideas and the exchange of thoughts. It is up to you if you are going to be the maximizer or minimizer of these opportunities. Making people feel comfortable sharing their thoughts by listening, engaging them, being trusted, being respectful, and reflecting is what the best do well.

Be a Polished Communicator

One of the first events that Tony Conway's company booked was a wedding. During the planning process, he met with the future bride, along with her mother and father. They met in the lobby of a local hotel, and after speaking to the family, the father of the bride looked down at Tony's scuffed shoes and said to him, "I hope your events are more polished than your shoes." This statement had a profound impact on the way Tony does business. To this day, he polishes his shoes every morning. He also keeps a shoe polish brush in his office so he can touch up his shoes if they get scuffed.[12]

This story provides a great metaphor for the importance of being a polished communicator. First impressions are important. You communicate with your appearance whether you realize it or not. When you are meeting someone for the first time, before you say even one word, that person will have already made certain judgments and created preconceived ideas about the type of person you are. Tony could have promised that father of the

You communicate with your appearance whether you realize it or not.

bride the world, but the father had already formed an opinion based on Tony's unpolished shoes. As communicators, the best understand that they have to take into account the message they send with not just with their words but also with their clothes, hair, body language, and every other nonverbal cue. These all have meaning, and they all send powerful statements to the person with whom you are communicating.

Tony learned a valuable lesson years ago, and to this day, his shoes are always polished to perfection. The same needs to be true of your communication. Every detail of what you plan to say and how you plan to say it must be polished to perfection. But don't forget that you also have to touch things up sometimes.

Let's say you had a great meeting with a potential client, and you polished and perfected your communication plan beforehand. You were dressed appropriately, early for the meeting, prepared to discuss the topic at hand, engaged with the other person, and listened. Your shoes were glistening, and the meeting went brilliantly. Now it is time for you to touch things up. Always follow up great communication with more great communication. I always tell my employees that the meeting really starts when you leave the meeting. Send the other person an e-mail thanking her for the meeting, or a phone call letting her know how much you appreciated her time. Better yet, send her more ideas that stem from your discussion. In other words, start working for potential clients before you actually get hired by them. Give them a taste of what it would be like to be your client. These small touch-ups show your attention to detail and that you were truly listening, and they are something that all the best communicators do as a matter of course. Lay a strong foundation for your communication, and touch it up often. It takes little effort but makes an enormous difference.

I do three simple things during the communication process to make sure it is as polished as possible: repeat, reach out, and reemphasize. I repeat what I heard to the other person before we part ways. It does not matter what we are talking about; I always boil it down in an effort to ensure we heard the same thing and to make certain that they know I was listening to what they had to say. Next, I reach out to them. I send an e-mail or call them to let them know I am thinking about our potential relationship. If we were talking about baseball, I send them an interesting article about a player or the team they expressed interest in. This allows me to create a link in their mind between our discussion and something that is important to them. Finally, I reemphasize. I act as if I have the business before I actually have the business. In other words, I continue to communicate through my actions and words how important this opportunity to work for them is to us.

These lessons are easy to implement: be polished, and always touch it up by repeating, reaching out, and reemphasizing. This will allow you to remain relevant to the other person, while solidifying your position and ultimately helping you reach your goal.

Tell Stories

Stories are powerful and easy to remember. When you communicate through real-life experiences or anecdotes, people are more inclined to engage and commit to the process. Stories are interesting, evoke emotions, and have the ability to strike a chord in someone's heart. People engage in things that pique their interest, and stories do just that. The best know the clout that stories offer and use them often. Think about the times you have heard a great motivational or business speaker. I am willing to bet that more often than not, that person began and ended with a story (and probably dropped several in between). Stories are the medium through which great communicators share ideas. This is because people have trouble remembering facts, but they can always repeat a great story.

When you communicate through stories, you give others the opportunity to identify with your message, absorb it, and repeat it as if it was their own. This identifying, digesting, and repeating are what make stories so effective. Speakers, friends, colleagues, and teammates share stories every day, and the reason is that they bring life to an issue. That is the power of the story as a communicative technique.

There is an old story floating around that when Lou Gerstner, former CEO of IBM, took over the company, he implemented a new strategy in his boardrooms. Instead of the endless presentations and slides that sucked the life out of the meetings, he decided that the best thing his executives could do would be to sit down with each other and tell stories. In the years during which Gerstner headed IBM, the company completely reinvented itself and regained its position as a relevant and cutting-edge company. This started from the top and worked its way down. Gerstner understood the power of stories and the value of turning facts into anecdotes.[13]

To communicate with as much impact as possible, use stories when you speak to others—those from your own life and experiences as well as those you've heard from others. It doesn't matter where the stories come from as long as they are relevant to the topic and make your point. You will immediately see a new interest in your message. The best know the enormous selling potential of stories and use this technique whenever they can.

See Things Through

The best communicators don't put up roadblocks during communication. They keep things connected and moving toward a solution. I always say, "Stay in the pain." It does not matter how difficult a situation may seem or how frustrating the communication may be, the best keep cool and remain dedicated to seeing it through. When it comes to communication, you have to remain dedicated to the process. Otherwise the communication process will fail.

Joe Theismann, the former NFL quarterback and a current commentator, has a great story about the results of dedicated communication:

> In 1981, when Hall of Fame Coach Joe Gibbs took over the Washington Redskins, we started off the season a miserable 0–5. Rumors began to swirl that Coach Gibbs wanted to trade me. This did not concern me. What concerned me was turning around our terrible start. At the time, I was always out and about in the city. I owned a restaurant and was involved in a lot of non-football-related opportunities. These rumors continued to progress, and I knew I had to do something. I remained concerned about the rumors and the lack of direct conversation between Coach and me. So after a loss, I drove over to Coach Gibbs's house and said, "Coach, we need to talk." Coach Gibbs told me, "Joe, I need a quarterback who is 100 percent dedicated to football."

> We spoke for awhile that day and flushed everything [out into the open]. . . . That year we won eight out of the next eleven, won the Super Bowl the following year, and made it to the Super Bowl the next. I was elected MVP [Most Valuable Player] of the league in 1984 under Coach Gibbs. I really feel that if I had not gone over there that day and had not spoken to Coach Gibbs, I could have been traded. I know that focusing my energy on both communicating with Coach Gibbs and removing outside distractions from my life made all of the difference in my career at the time.[14]

This is what the best do. Even when things aren't going well, they stay in the game and remain dedicated to the communication process. From the hello to the good-bye to the follow-up, each piece is a valuable part of the puzzle. Their dedication fuels their drive to succeed as communicators. Joe went directly to his coach's house to work through the issues they were having. Things weren't going well, but he had enough pride in himself; respect for his teammates, fans, and community; and confidence in the end result to stay in it and work through it. If he had avoided a difficult conversation, who knows what would have happened? But his dedication to the communication process and his respect for his team laid the foundation for one of the greatest teams in NFL history.

When it comes to communication, you cannot give up: the more important the relationship is to you, the more important it is to stay in it through any tough times. First and foremost, you have to be involved and engaged. Don't let your own frustration or the frustration of others deter you from your goals of connecting and forming relationships. Others may try to derail you, but you have to stay on track and keep moving in the right direction.

Conclusion

Communication is a process. Just like with anything else in life, you have to nurture it, care for it, and remain engaged for results to occur. No one style works for everyone every time because each person and situation is unique. But there are steps that each of us can take to improve our ability to communicate. You must remain dedicated to the process and see things through to the end regardless of any difficulties. You must also approach the process with an open and curious mind, treat others and their ideas respectfully, and be certain that you and your own ideas are prepared and polished. Paying attention to these elements will improve your communication style, which will help you both personally and professionally, and put you on track to becoming one of the best communicators.

4

Develop Your Likability

All things being equal, people will do business with, and refer business to, those people they know, like, and trust.
—Bob Burg

We all want to be liked. It is human nature to strive to become the type of person who attracts others. And the quality of the people with whom we surround ourselves has an enormous effect on our own life. Often your likability helps define your professional and personal success. When you are likable, you will always have a friend or colleague you can reach out to for help, guidance, and advice.

To be likable, you do not have to be an athlete, or top business executive, or even someone with a really interesting job. You do not have to try to entertain people by being unbelievably funny or having a repertoire of great stories. These are not the things that make a person likable. In fact, the most likable people don't necessarily set out to be liked or try very hard at all. For many lucky people, being likable is just who they are.

Nonetheless, likability is a skill that almost anyone can learn. And even if you are already likable, you can develop that skill even more. Likability is imperative to finding success in business. People who like you will want to work with you. In addition, they will work harder to support you even if they normally would not do the same for others. Being likable increases your ability to be successful.

The basis of likability is understanding what draws you to other people and implementing those qualities and characteristics in your relationships. This chapter focuses on identifying those characteristics and presenting them in a way that makes them easy to learn.

Five Ways to Develop Your Likability

I have separated likability into five basic pieces. I call them mantras because you need to remind yourself of them over and over:

1. Be authentic.
2. If you are going to do it, give it 100 percent.
3. Be optimistic and energetic.
4. Use 360-degree awareness.
5. Exceed expectations.

If you constantly remind yourself of these five mantras and practice them, they will create a magnetic effect that will attract others to you in a powerful way.

Mantra 1: Be Authentic

The most likable people in the world are authentic. They are dedicated to their personal values and character, so much so that their actions mirror their thoughts and beliefs at all times. They are who they say they are, and they never act in a way that is inconsistent with their core beliefs.

People want to surround themselves with others who are genuine. They want you to really be who you say you are, who you appear to be. When I began interviewing some of the best for this book, I quickly learned that they believed in the importance of authenticity. As I interviewed athletes, coaches, broadcasters, CEOs, and businesspeople, one of the most commonly referenced notions was that to be liked requires being authentic. More important, to be successful, you have to maintain an authenticity that people can see, hear, and sense.

As a young boy, the esteemed broadcaster Ernie (EJ) Johnson Jr. dreamed of becoming a broadcaster, following in the footsteps of his father, Ernie Johnson Sr., a successful broadcaster in his own day. When Ernie was young, his father gave him what he considered to be the most important advice he has ever received. His father told him, "To be successful, be yourself." EJ believes to this day that you cannot change your style to cater to someone else. He said, "If you are true to yourself, you will never feel that you have to perform or be something that you are not."

Ernie has found that when people who have seen him on television approach him in public and talk to him, they will say in a puzzled way after a few minutes of conversation, "You are the same in person as you are on television." "It's the funniest thing," EJ muses. "Of course, I am. That is me on TV." He believes that the reason his National Basketball Association (NBA) analysis show on TNT, with Charles Barkley and Kenny Smith, is successful is that all three of them are being themselves. None of them acts for the camera or tries to be something they are not. They do not rehearse, and they let their thoughts, feelings, and character shine through in the show. It's also no coincidence that Ernie's *Inside the NBA* has become an Emmy Award–winning show.[1] The best know that to succeed, you need to be yourself.

The best know that to succeed, you need to be yourself.

I've often heard the saying that perception is reality, meaning that who people perceive you to be is who you are in their mind, even though that perception may be inaccurate. The best understand this and ensure that their actions reflect their character so that the perception others have of them is correct. However, the best place just as much emphasis on the converse of this statement. They flip the concept entirely to be that reality should be perception. This is the core concept behind authenticity. It means that who you really are is how people should perceive you because you are not trying to be something you are not.

Speaker and author Bob Burg believes that "one thing that leads to likability is you don't try to be someone that you are not. You stay within your true character and you do not put on a facade."[2] It truly is as easy as it sounds. There is no mystery, and the biggest obstacles are being comfortable with yourself and coming to terms with the fundamental idea that people will like and appreciate you for exactly who you are. And if they figure out you are putting on an act for their friendship, they will not want to be around you. When it comes to being authentic, you create your own destiny. Stay true to yourself, and others will be true to you as well. It is not about getting people to buy into you or even selling yourself to others. If you are genuine and honest with yourself, people will naturally be attracted to both you and your energy.

Mantra 2: If You Are Going to Do It, Give It 100 Percent

If you commit to something, give it your all. Whether it comes in the form of attention, effort, or consideration, the most likable people offer others what they may not even offer themselves (but should): 100 percent. They do not cut corners, and once they commit, they see things through. If you commit to something but don't follow through or do it in a halfhearted way, you will disappoint people at best and anger them at worst. Unfortunately, people often do not give others all that they have. They instead give a distracted, busy, disinterested, or lazy version of themselves. That is certainly no way to go about connecting with others. If you commit, do what you promised, and do it well. If you can't do it, don't commit. Or if something changes, communicate the change and work toward a mutually beneficial solution. Pretty simple.

Edie Fraser is the senior consultant for a company that specializes in high-level recruitment services for leading businesses. She diligently works to promote diversity and the advancement of minorities and women in the most senior levels of corporations and organizations. When she met iconic news anchor Walter Cronkite for the first time, she was putting together an international media organization for the Peace Corps. This is how she recalled that meeting:

> I saw Mr. Cronkite at an event and approached him, asking him to be the chairman of this organization. He asked that I fly to New York and meet with him at the CBS headquarters. I made the trip, and when we met, after much discussion, he looked at me and told me he was sorry but he was about to disappoint me because it was the right thing to do. He explained that with the upcoming presidential election, he had to focus all of his energy covering it and said he did not believe in just giving his name, as he felt you have to be devoted to your cause 100 percent when you commit. While I was greatly disappointed, I respected his dedication and communication. I have grown to admire his decision, and even today, I make sure that when I commit, I give 100 percent.[3]

Cronkite was one of the most successful news broadcasters of the twentieth century and covered some of the most important events of the time. He had a likability about him that few others have managed to achieve; in fact, he was commonly referred to as "Uncle Walter." Part of this likability is evidenced in Edie's experience with him: if he could not do something fully, he did not care to do it at all.

To be a success in life, you have to give it all of your effort and your energy. This is the attitude that likable people have toward life. Simply knowing that someone is giving you all he or she can provides comfort. This dedication needs to permeate every facet of your life. When you listen, you must focus; when you act, do so with effort; and when you promise, you must deliver.

John Wooden is one of the most famous basketball coaches to have ever lived. He won ten championships over a twelve-year period while coaching at UCLA. The iconic Wooden once said, "Nothing will work unless you do." This statement truly encompasses the importance of effort. At the end of the day, you get out what you put in. But even more important to you and your legacy, when it comes to helping others and dedicating yourself to their cause, other people also get out what you put in. If you want to be successful, people must like you, which means it is your responsibility to give everything you have when you dedicate yourself to others. People will appreciate you, value you, and like you because you tried for them like no one else ever tried before.

Mantra 3: Be Optimistic and Energetic

The most likable individuals are positive, optimistic, and energetic, and they diligently work to draw people in with an attitude that is upbeat and affirming. In short, they try to lift people up and make them smile, even when others may not want to smile. Edie Fraser admitted that she is a hugger and cannot help it because she overflows with warmth: "I remember going into a very important meeting in a global government situation with a group of people. As the meeting concluded, I began thanking another woman in the room and reached out and hugged her. Someone turned to me and told me that we don't hug here. Well, that is not me, and I stood behind my hug as I am one to show positive feelings and embrace others whenever

I have the chance."[4] While it is always important to ensure you respect others' boundaries and remain sensitive to their feelings, positive energy and demonstrating a good attitude will almost always result in good feelings all around.

Bob Burg believes that "likability is focusing on making people feel good about themselves in a genuine way."[5] People respond to optimism and positive energy, magnetic qualities that draw others in. When they leave a conversation or an interaction feeling warmth and positive energy, they are more responsive and will feel a fundamental likability toward you. It is important to maintain a positive attitude and outlook in life. Throughout our journey, we all will face personal obstacles and experiences that will challenge us mentally and physically. We will lose jobs, relationships will end, friendships will grow stale, opportunities may be missed, and goals may not be reached. Sometimes the only thing you can control during difficult times is your reaction and your attitude.

Focus on the controllables.

When I was growing up, my parents always told me, "Focus on the controllables." I always tell my clients and the people with whom I work the same thing. There are things we can control and things we cannot, no matter how hard we try. The ultimate controllables in life are your choices and your attitude, and the best know that above all else.

No one wants to be around someone with a bad attitude. Think about your closest friends and colleagues. I am willing to bet part of the reason you love many of them and enjoy their company is their energy and contagious optimism. The best and most likable people understand the power of optimism and the meaningful way it complements and compounds likability. Few unenergetic pessimists win over people's hearts and minds. But if you have a contagious energy, a welcoming attitude, and a generally likable personality, you can and will.

Winston Churchill said, "A pessimist sees the difficulty in every opportunity; an optimist sees the opportunity in every difficulty." One of my favorite stories about optimism in the face of difficult times is about Jim Valvano, a former coach of North Carolina State University's men's basketball team. Jim won the 1983 National Collegiate Athletic Association basketball championship against all odds and became an instant celebrity, remembered for his endless enthusiasm and energy. Nine years later, in 1992, he was diagnosed with terminal cancer and was told that he had a very limited time to live.

Jim and his family were devastated. Jim's response was, "I can choose to live, or wait to die." As the optimist he was, Jim chose to live his life fully during the time he had left. With ESPN, Jim started the V Foundation for Cancer Research, a philanthropic organization that gives the money it raises to fund research to find cures for cancer. Jim passed away ten months after he was diagnosed, but through his optimism and attitude toward his situation, he made a difference. Since its start in 1993, the V Foundation for Cancer Research has raised almost $100 million to fund cancer research. It started with one man who saw the opportunity in his own personal battle.[6]

Part of likability is tied to how you handle difficult situations. The sports community was drawn into Jim's battle because he was so optimistic and positive. Everyone around him respected the way that he carried himself in the face of life's most difficult obstacle—and even loved him for it. Jim's spirit lives on through his foundation and the money it raises to find cures for cancer. It all started with a positive attitude toward a devastating situation.

When it comes to difficult experiences, all we can do is control our reactions and our attitudes. Becoming more likable is just one effect of having a positive attitude. Being optimistic is truly life altering. Every big idea and dream starts with a good attitude and enthusiasm.

People are drawn to optimism and enthusiasm. The more they get it, the more they have a desire for it. It is up to you to be a positive person who draws others in. Your likability stems from your own behavior.

Mantra 4: Use 360-Degree Awareness

The phrase "360-degree awareness" means that you are fully aware of people and their needs and understand those needs even before they are voiced. People like others who are informed, engaged, and sensitive to their wants, and then hustle to make their lives easier. When you are fully aware, you become more thoughtful and insightful—something people appreciate and like.

I have three daughters. When one of my daughters was in the hospital due to an emergency, my next-door neighbor swooped in to take care of our other two daughters: babysitting, cooking dinner, helping them with homework, and creating some sense of a normal life for them while my husband and I spent most of our days and nights at the hospital. Not once did I ask my neighbor for her help or support; she was just there. She knew what we needed and jumped in to help my family. There were no questions asked, no recommendations made, and nothing but action and results. She gave me the inner comfort I needed so I could better focus on helping my hospitalized daughter, and this meant the world to us. This is what I mean by 360-degree awareness: offering a solution before someone tells you the problem.

Let's revisit Jim Valvano. When Jim was coaching at North Carolina State, his female counterpart was Kay Yow, one of the most successful coaches in women's basketball, with over seven hundred wins to her name. After she was diagnosed with breast cancer in 1987 during one of her seasons at NC State, Jim called her one day during the peak of the basketball season and said he was coming over to say hello. She tried to persuade him not to come, knowing how valuable his time was and how horrible she was feeling, but Jim would not take no for an answer. When he showed up, it was with his entire staff and a full meal catered by a local Italian restaurant. They did everything, from setup to cleanup, not allowing Kay to do a thing. Instead they talked about school and what was going on because Yow had been away for some time. Kay reminisced, "Just to have the thought to do something like that is special. I know basketball coaches and the schedule that a basketball coach and an athletic director has is very busy. There is an overwhelming amount of time spent and to take two hours out of any day with your entire staff is something extraordinary. It takes a special person just to think about doing something like that to begin with and then follow through with it."[7]

This story truly encompasses the spirit of 360-degree awareness. It is about doing things for others even when they may tell you they don't need it or they don't want it to be done.

It goes back to Ernie Johnson Jr. and his "just click Send" mentality. Above and beyond anything else, people appreciate when you step up. Part of being likable means understanding the power of being aware and being involved in others' lives. It is about making a conscious effort and thinking about what others need and how you can help.

This awareness starts by looking into people's lives and listening to what they have to say when you speak with them. People love to talk about themselves, and if you give them the opportunity, they will give you all you need to know. Then it is up to you to create a plan. I always consider the "three whats" when I try to help others:

1. What is the situation?
2. What do they need?
3. What can I do to help?

If you ask yourself these three questions and come up with answers, you will know exactly what you can do. These basic questions are the backbone of 360-degree awareness. Start with them, and see where they take you.

Being aware of the people around you will help you form relationships and turn those relationships into potentially lifelong friendships. The best know that this is done through looking at all angles of someone else's life so you can find a way to improve that life. These actions result in a likability that cannot be faked, reproduced, or imitated.

Mantra 5: Exceed Expectations

Maintaining a 360-degree awareness of others helps to ensure that you know what people really need. But you want to do more than meet these needs; you want to exceed them. Set goals you know for certain you can meet, but then blow past them. This is about focusing on how you can give people more than they expect to receive.

Almost everyone has heard the story about the big bucket and the rocks. After filling a large bucket to the brim with rocks, a teacher looks at his young student and asks if the bucket is full. The student says that he believes it is. So then the teacher proceeds to dump cup after cup of smaller rocks into the bucket, filling the crevices the larger rocks created. He then asks the young student if he now believes the bucket is full. The student once again says yes. So now the teacher proceeds to pour cup after cup of sand into the bucket, filling the crevices between the smaller rocks. The student says once again the bucket is definitely full. Then the teacher pours water into the bucket.

This is how I look at expectations. People expect you to fill their bucket with big rocks until it can hold no more. These big rocks are the phone calls when someone is sick, supportive e-mails when someone has a big presentation, and the inspirational quotes and thoughts you send someone who is up for a promotion. These are the things that most people will do. But the best go one, two, and even three steps further. The best give others the small rocks, the sand, and the water. They find room in those buckets that others don't see.

The small rocks may be a personal visit or taking time out of your busy schedule, essentially going the extra step. The sand could be bringing others their favorite dinner or flowers with you as an expression of good wishes. The water is taking it even further and filling people's buckets and exceeding their expectations: it may be by helping others to prepare for a tough presentation or taking your sick friend for treatment and staying with him or her during that time. In each instance, it is about raising the bar and going further than you thought possible. There is no limit to giving, and the more expectations you exceed, the better. Whatever the case, there are always ways to take people's expectations and blow them out of the water.

It is not just about putting the big rocks, or the small ones, or even the sand and the water in the bucket. That is the easy part. Once you figure out what people's expectations are, it is easy to meet and exceed them. But what separates the best from everyone else is the ability to see the crevices—to see the opportunity to put more in the bucket. It is the idea that when others see no more that can be done, you see all the opportunity that remains.

Ernie Johnson Jr. works hard as a philanthropist, and when he helps others, he blows away their expectations by taking his efforts to the next level. While working at the 2009 NBA All Star Game, Ernie befriended a young boy from Dallas who had non-Hodgkin's lymphoma, the same disease Ernie had had. The boy was a guest of the Make-A-Wish-Foundation, and his wish was to meet his favorite player from Dallas, Dirk Nowitzki. Ernie stayed in touch with the boy after that weekend. The next year, the All Star Game was in Dallas. Ernie was covering the game, and when he was given two tickets, he called the boy and invited him to the event. At the game, Ernie bumped into the NBA representative who works with Make-A-Wish and told her about the boy at the game. She made sure that the young boy got to spend a few minutes with Dirk again. This young boy, who was suffering from a terrible illness, had the opportunity to attend a dream game and to meet his hero twice.[8]

This is what exceeding expectations is all about: going as far as you can go for other people. A young boy facing a terrible prognosis was given the gift of happiness: a few successful men with a great platform and an opportunity to make a difference exceeded this boy's expectations.

I always tell my employees and clients not to meet people's expectations but to beat them. Be like a booming stock in a bull market. Shatter your projected earnings statements. Exceeding expectations is a reflection of not only your effort but your sensitivity to others and their situations. This will help you increase your ability to form relationships and friendships. You will become more likable for the simple fact that people know you care enough to take the extra step.

The Power of Likability

The most likable people in the world know that these five simple things make people more valuable to others and therefore more likable. And when people like you, I say, "they will want to help you." Being likable is about authentically investing in others. Once you focus your time and effort on how others feel, you not only increase your likability but you benefit the human race and spirit. We all need strong relationships and well-built support systems, and

> *Being likable is about authentically investing in others.*

thinking about and caring for others helps build a strong foundation for both. Likability is a natural side effect of these efforts.

I am a firm believer that when people do not like you, you can do no right, and when people like you, you can do no wrong. What it comes down to is that developing your likability is about forming relationships and investing in people. Bob Burg told me, "In life, you have to make your win about other people's win. And when you do that, they want to see you succeed and they want to be part of your life and are much more about your mission." It is a simple yet profound concept. Start with the five mantras:

- Be authentic in the way you act and the things you say.
- Give people 100 percent, regardless of the situation, and they will value you and your effort.
- Be optimistic. People will appreciate your positive energy, and it will make you approachable.
- Be aware. Focus on others, and be aware of their needs and desires. Invest in their lives, and figure out what you can do to help.
- Exceed expectations. Shoot for the stars, and work hard to not only understand what people need but offer them more.

If you implement these five ideologies into your everyday life, you will become more likable and people will be drawn to you. The best part is that once they begin to like you, they will want to form relationships with you, introduce you to their friends, network for you, help you, and be invested in your life.

And the more people you have invested in your life, the better your chances are of being successful.

The best don't do it alone. They have supporters, enthusiasts, investors, coaches, and friends and colleagues tied firmly to their success. This is because they form relationships and friendships, and at the end of the day, they are given business opportunities because people like and respect them. And they like and respect them because the best give others what they deserve: authenticity, effort, dedication, and sincerity.

5

Give Back

Each of us can be a rainbow of hope, doing what we can to extend ourselves in kindness and grace to one another. And I know for sure that there is no them, there's only us.

—Oprah Winfrey

The best have the desire and the ability to make a difference. Whether it is by supporting a cause that they are passionate about or finding a way to offer others the same success and opportunities that they have had, they feel a personal responsibility to reach out and improve the communities and people who surround and support their businesses. Giving back is about building and strengthening communities. It is about interacting with and forming relationships with those you help. When your community is thriving, the people who live there are better able to support you and your business. And if you help them thrive, not only will they be able to support you, they will want to. When society at large succeeds, we all succeed. The best know that by working to become a lifeline and support system for others, they create a prosperous and flourishing economy for everyone to be a part of.

Part of the reason that the most successful people reach peaks in both their personal and professional lives is that they help others. They do not simply reach peaks; they take others with them on their way up. They drive people to reach higher personal goals. The best are enablers in the most positive sense. They enable others to do better, reach higher, and achieve more. Helping and enabling others means more than helping individuals they know reach their goals. It also means providing for the less fortunate and giving them the opportunity to better themselves and find their own success.

The best are enablers in the most positive sense. They enable others to do better, reach higher, and achieve more.

We can all look to our communities and see where the need may be. Ultimately we have a responsibility to improve the lives of others with the resources available to us.

Think about how many great scholars, public servants, businesspeople, athletes, and entertainers grew up in poverty: Oprah Winfrey, J. K. Rowling, John D. Rockefeller—the list goes on and on. All of their success stories started with one thing: an opportunity. And many of these opportunities came from someone who was successful in his or her own trade and wanted to reach out and influence a better tomorrow.

The best know how to use their resources to create a better world for the rest of us. And just as when it comes to communicating, negotiating, and the other lessons in this book, the go-getters approach giving back in the same manner: with direction, unique insight, and a dedication to the end result of making a difference.

So how can you give back to others for the greater good?

Listen to Your Inner Voice

Giving back starts from within. We all have an inner voice that reflects what we value and cherish. It helps motivate our actions and leads us down our chosen paths in life. The best listen to that voice. I have noted in this book the importance of undertaking endeavors you are passionate about, and the same is true when it comes to giving back. No endeavor will be productive and successful if it is not anchored inside you. Charitable actions have to be focused on something that you believe in, so that you will put your time and energy into them. You cannot adopt someone else's belief system or values. The best find a need that relates to their inner voice and beliefs.

When my daughter was in the hospital after an injury, we were fortunate to have received the unparalleled support and care that Children's Healthcare of Atlanta provided for her. As a member of the board at Children's, I was passionate about supporting the hospital even before my daughter's injury. After my family's personal experience, my passion to help has become a daily mission to give in order to help other children.

Philanthropic organizations often approach athletes and ask them to join their cause and support the foundation in its fundraising activities. When this happens to my clients, we always discuss these opportunities. After reviewing the charity, I ask my client, "Does this organization resonate with you? Does the cause mean anything to you? Do you identify with it?" I ask these questions because if they are going to commit their name and their efforts to a cause, they need to be committed to and passionate about it so that they will put their energy into it and get results.

Mike Maroth, a Major League Baseball (MLB) player, listened to his inner voice while playing for the Detroit Tigers. His father had been diagnosed with multiple sclerosis, and Mike viewed his status as a professional athlete as a platform from which he could give back. He worked closely with the Tigers and aligned with a local charity to have a National MS Day at the Detroit Tigers ballpark. He also enlisted the help of his teammates and a local bowling alley to sell lanes to individuals and businesses that wanted to support the cause. Those who purchased lanes would have the opportunity to bowl with some of their favorite Detroit Tigers players. The goal was to raise fifty to seventy-five thousand dollars, and Mike did just that. The Tigers also gave Mike's father the opportunity to fulfill a lifelong dream and throw the first pitch of a game.

This is exactly what I mean by following your inner voice. Find a way to give back that resonates with you, and then pursue it. The best give, and they focus on the causes that they believe in because they understand that we succeed in giving only when we are passionate about a cause. Everyone has an inner voice and can relate to a need. Your responsibility is to decide exactly what need you want to fulfill and then get moving.

Change Your Thinking About Giving

Many people view charitable giving as a tax write-off or a way to ease their conscience. The best know it is much more than that. They do not look at giving as a burden or job requirement or a break on their taxes. For the best, making a difference is a joy and a pleasure that benefits others and themselves as well.

Bob Burg believes that "giving back implies you first took something from someone. Even the term 'pay it forward' indicates you had to get something first before you could give. This indicates that you just did not first add value to someone's life. It leads to the conclusion that you gave back or gave forward because you owed something to someone. That is why I just leave it at nothing more than 'giving.'"[1] This is the fundamental heartbeat of giving back: don't think of it as some sort of payment or repayment; view it as something truly altruistic.

Giving is a choice, and every little bit makes a difference. Even a few hours of volunteer work can change lives. I spent a great deal of time at Children's Healthcare after my daughter's injury and noticed the many small things that made the hospital so special. There were book carts, video games, toys, stuffed animals, and numerous other small touches that made this environment more comfortable and comforting for young patients. It became evident to me that children thrive more in a children's hospital environment than in one specializing in adult treatment. These small touches inspired me to focus on the ability to make a difference even on a small level. Many people think that when it comes to charity, their contribution will not make a difference. In fact, when it comes to philanthropy, we can all make a difference. You only have to ask the child who used the paper or the arts and crafts supplies someone gave to the hospital or the sick child who had hope and kept fighting because of a donation that helped fund a volunteer dog to come to his bedside and make him smile or reach his arms forward to pet the dog, something the therapist has struggled to get him to do. It is easy for anyone to give a children's hospital a few books for the book cart, a new video game for the systems the hospital has, or even a new toy or stuffed animal, making a small difference in the lives of many children. As the old saying goes, little things make a big difference.

The best know that giving is about more than the money. Stedman Graham, an educator, businessman, author, and motivational speaker, runs a successful management and marketing consultation company. He is also the founder of several philanthropic foundations focused on giving back and community development. One of these foundations, AAD Education, Health and Sports, is a nonprofit that works with numerous professional athletes and civic leaders to infuse leadership and mentoring in underdeveloped communities. The foundation has donated over $1.5 million in scholarships to young people.[2] It is his belief that "there is so much more you can give than money. It takes just as long to learn how to give as it does to learn how to run a successful business. The key is a work/life balance, and to understand that, you can learn just as much from community service as you can from getting a master's degree at a major university. You simply do yourself a disservice when you don't give back."[3]

Giving, just like any other life experience, is something you can learn and something that can help you become a better person personally and professionally. I have seen many of my clients choose to give time instead of or in addition to money. I found out that John Smoltz, the former MLB pitcher, used to go to the hospital, walk in unannounced, and ask a nurse if there was a group of children who were having a particularly tough time. He would then spend time with the children, play with them, bring them gifts, and sign autographs for them. Other of my clients have delivered turkeys to people for Thanksgiving. Regardless of who they are or how they choose to give their time, they all tell me that giving time offers something that giving money does not—a learning experience and a personal exchange between individuals.

The education you gain from your philanthropic endeavors may be the most valuable part of the process. Ernie Johnson Jr. notes:

> The people I admire the most and who are really the great examples for the rest of us are those who use their opportunities to empower other people. But when you do this, you cannot be tied to the outcome, you have to be enthusiastic about the experience and ability to learn from the process. . . . I have adopted four children. We do not know what the outcome will be when we do this. If I said I had to have an outcome on this a certain way, we would be missing out on the opportunity to give a chance to and learn from these beautiful children.[4]

Giving offers you the opportunity to surround yourself with people from different walks of life with various life experiences and diverse backgrounds. Each person whose life you touch will offer you the ability to learn. When it comes to giving, it is not just about the outcome or end result; rather the value lies in the process of giving itself. The best know that by giving to others and opening up our hearts and minds, we can also learn from others. By giving, we create an opportunity to not only better the lives of others but to better our own lives as well.

By giving, we create an opportunity to not only better the lives of others but to better our own lives as well.

Giving Starts Locally

Some people believe that philanthropy is purely a global project, but it can be equally as effective, and maybe more so, when it is targeted and local. It really all starts with one person doing one good deed for one person in need financially, physically, or even emotionally. The best begin by listening to their inner voice and looking for a need they can fulfill. And since the easiest place to begin looking is in your own backyard, that is what they do. They start locally. The following two examples of charity and philanthropy started locally, and they've made a difference.

Two Dozen Flowers

Ernie Johnson Jr. and his wife, Cheryl, have six children. Whenever he goes to the supermarket, his kids always want to go with him because of a giving game that they play as they leave the supermarket. When leaving the store, they buy two bouquets of flowers: one bouquet they take home to his wife, Cheryl, and the other bouquet they give to a random person in the parking lot. During each trip, a different person gets to decide who will get the flowers, and they scan the parking lot until they see someone they think could benefit from the bouquet that day.

Just before Christmas one year, it was Ernie's turn to choose. He saw a woman sitting alone in her car with the engine running and looking distracted. Ernie decided she could use the flowers, so he and his children approached the car and knocked on the window. When she opened it, he explained that they had purchased two bouquets of flowers. One was for his wife, Cheryl, so they had an extra bouquet and thought she might like it. Her eyes welled up with tears at his words, and she said, "Thank you so much for this. My husband died two weeks ago, and I never thought I would get another bouquet of roses again." Ernie knew that giving people flowers for no reason would probably surprise and please them, but after hearing this woman's words, he was stunned. He was also filled with warmth knowing that his small gesture of kindness made a huge difference in the life of someone who really needed some caring for.[5]

This small act of kindness likely brightened that woman's day, and maybe even week or month. Ernie and his family implemented this small but thoughtful mission as a reminder to others that people care about them and they matter. This task betters the community in which Ernie and his family reside through the fact that they bring people happiness. It is easy to offer someone a bouquet of roses, and it may make a memorable and important difference in their life.

Offering a Mentor

Stedman Graham founded AAD Education, Health and Sports, a nonprofit, philanthropic organization with over five hundred professional athletes and other civic leaders committed to developing leadership in underserved youth. AAD has served over fifteen thousand underprivileged students through scholarships and education, many of them from Chicago, where he now lives.

Graham himself was raised in an underprivileged community with few, if any, opportunities, but was fortunate to meet people who helped him and helped change his life. He understands that "it takes a whole lot of people to make a change in a child's life," and so he founded AAD Education to teach young people how to find their personal identity. AAD's goal is to help children build a strong foundation that will help them succeed in life. It offers underprivileged youth the chance to work with mentors and athletes across America to curb drug use, energize themselves, and get on the fast track to success. Graham believes that "everyone is looking for hope. If you can just be in that space to offer them hope, teach them how to play golf, offer them an organization with a homework club, or perhaps an after-school extracurricular activity, that may be all they need to uplift themselves and make a difference in their own personal lives.

"Volunteering inspires more volunteering," Graham continues. Some of the young people who have gone through the AAD programs have been inspired to volunteer as mentors in AAD or elsewhere themselves. They want to make a difference in the lives of others, just as others have made a difference in their lives.[6]

Because Graham himself had to fight to succeed in life and was fortunate enough to receive help along the way, he is passionate about helping others have those same opportunities. By looking locally, he found that there were plenty of opportunities to help underprivileged youth get ahead by giving them the support they may not otherwise have.

The best understand the importance of giving back to the community. Whether it is the simple act of finding someone who could use a dozen roses or diligently working to change someone's life by offering them guidance and direction, these acts of kindness strengthen a community and offer hope and opportunity where they may not have otherwise been present.

Corporate Giving

Giving to others is not something that the best do just in their personal lives. The best businesses and their top executives recognize the value of giving back to the communities that surround them. The fundamental concept is that a healthy and sustainable community promotes and supports a flourishing and successful business, so helping the community helps the business, thereby creating a mutually advantageous relationship, with both parties reaping the benefits. Interestingly enough, this has not always been a priority for businesses and executives. It always used to be, "How much can we make?" But now, executives are shifting, and business culture has seen a considerable tilt toward asking, "How much can we give?"

Over seventeen hundred global CEOs and business leaders and their businesses collectively account for more than 40 percent of reported corporate giving in the United States.[7]

These companies are putting more than $14 billion a year into charitable causes. In a recent poll by the Committee Encouraging Corporate Philanthropy, the only international forum of business leaders focused on corporate philanthropy of leading CEOs and giving officers, a clear majority in both groups reported that they believe it is necessary to take a proactive approach to solving social problems that affect their business.[8] These social problems can range from people in need of food and water in the community to better educational programs. The overwhelming reason that corporations give is that once they begin to address social reform, they create a more prosperous economy for everyone.

Now, more than ever before, there is an internal focus in these large companies spearheaded by their top executives to give back to the community and find ways where they can make a difference. Many of these large corporations view their marketing strategy behind corporate giving in the same way they view their marketing strategy behind corporate earnings: as a means to a financial end. This is because top executives know that companies will die if their surrounding ecosystem does not flourish.

The best are innovative and razor sharp when it comes to leading the way and implementing cutting-edge business development. The CEOs and other top executives and leaders at these companies know that giving back is not just about the philanthropic results; it is about business results. As obvious as it sounds, people are more inclined to support businesses that they identify with. So when a corporation is working hard to raise money for a philanthropic organization with which you identify, it's likely that you will be more inclined to support that company. Building a strong philanthropic network is about forming relationships, identifying with the people who support your cause, and, most important, getting them to identify with you. Whether forming personal relationships or professional relationships with the community, the basic concept is the same: people want to work with those they like and they like those whom they relate to.

One of my favorite philanthropic endeavors came from Mickey Mouse himself. In 2010 Disney and the HandsOn Network, the largest volunteer network in the nation, began a philanthropic endeavor they called, "Give a Day, Get a Disney Day." Disney offered any person who completed a volunteer project a one-day free admission pass to a Disney park.[9] Within less than twelve weeks, over 1 million people had completed or committed to a service project. That means that 1 million people made a difference in the lives of at least 1 million other people, and probably twice that number, or even more. When millions of lives are changed through the strategic marketing and efforts of a large corporation, it becomes clear that corporate giving can have a huge effect on society at large.

This program offered people a chance to be rewarded for their kindness and charitable contributions, and it helped the community at large by inspiring those same people to take action and volunteer when they possibly otherwise may not have. From a purely business perspective, by giving these people free admission. Disney increased its attendance, and these park goers inevitably spent money throughout the park.

This truly demonstrates the win-win approach that giving back can offer both society at large and its businesses.

Corporate giving can take many forms. It may be something as seemingly simple as Disney's "Give a Day, Get a Disney Day," or it may be a corporation that is addressing a larger need in its own community. It also often starts when just one person in an organization believes in a cause or sees a need and aligns his or her inner voice with that need. This is what happened at the Children's Hospital of Atlanta.

In 1990, Vicki Riedel worked in fundraising at the Children's Hospital of Atlanta. Her daughter had leukemia, and she was frustrated by the fact that although she worked in a hospital in Atlanta, they had to go to Seattle multiple times so that her daughter could receive bone marrow transplants because none of the hospitals in Atlanta had a quality cancer center. Vicki wanted change but knew that she needed funding, so she approached Aflac Insurance, which is based in Georgia, and its CEO, Dan Amos, requesting a $25,000 donation to improve the cancer center at the hospital. However, after learning more about the global needs of the hospital relevant to this issue Amos volunteered to Vicki that Aflac would donate $3 million, funding that created the Aflac Cancer Center. Dan and Vicki worked together to recruit an expert on children's cancer, and eventually found Bill Woods, a well-respected physician specializing in pediatric oncology, who agreed to become director. But Aflac did not stop there: the organization has donated over $53 million to the center since its inception in 1995 because Woods quickly surmised that to make an impact much more was needed. Since then, other people and businesses have funded numerous rooms in the hospital as well. Together they have created a facility that treats more than 350 new cancer patients each year and follows more than 2,500 patients with sickle cell disease, hemophilia, and other blood disorders. The center has been recognized by *U.S. News and World Report* as one of the top childhood cancer centers in the country.[10] And it all began with one person's vision and the financial support of one company whose leader was driven to make a difference. Once that happened, others in the community stepped up and bought into the cause.[11]

The best understand their responsibility to improve society when the opportunity arises.

Children's Healthcare of Atlanta has an army of givers and talented people coming together to make a difference. Aflac's generous corporate giving enabled the creation of a powerhouse to treat and fight children's cancer. Without that support, the Aflac Cancer Center wouldn't exist and the children it treats would very likely have to travel far or settle for less effective treatment. This example demonstrates both the power and the importance of corporate philanthropy. Businesses have resources and finances that can make a difference, and when they do make a difference, everyone benefits. The best understand their responsibility to improve society when the opportunity arises, and that is just what Aflac and Dan Amos did.[12]

Caring Inspires Caring

Caring for others makes an enormous difference in our society. The added benefit of caring enough to make a difference is that caring often inspires more caring, creating a trickle-down effect. When other people see the go-getters and game changers diligently work to improve others' lives, they may be inspired to do the same. And when people are directly touched by another's generosity, they will most likely be motivated to pay it forward.

One person's care for another can move mountains. When you set about helping others, you will build relationships, friendships, and networking opportunities, which will help drive you to success in your business and personal life. Donna Hyland, the president and CEO of Children's Healthcare of Atlanta, works to change lives every day, and she is fortunate enough to see the result of her work. One such result came when Jessica Jones was treated at Children's. Jessica was fourteen years old in 2002 when she arrived at Children's. She had been playing with friends on Halloween and fell five feet off a porch onto solid concrete and severely injured her head. By the time the ambulance got her to the hospital, she was near death. The attending physician, Andrew Reisner, performed an emergency craniotomy, yet her chances of survival were less than 5 percent, and she was in a coma. Reisner felt that even if Jessica did survive and regain consciousness, she had a less than 10 percent chance of regaining full functionality. Five days later, she came out of her coma and began breathing on her own. Jessica had to relearn every function, including how to eat, walk, and read, yet after only two months, she returned to her high school honor classes. The following spring, Reisner sent her a letter that said, "I just want you to know how proud I am of you. And remember, this is your story." That letter and her experience inspired Jessica to begin volunteering at Children's. Eventually she went to Stanford University, and in 2010, she graduated from Stanford with honors and went on to Yale to work on a master's degree in human biology and begin a research fellowship in neuroscience. Jessica and her family have retained close ties with Reisner and Children's, and a few years ago, Jessica's mother, Leslie Jones, an attorney in Atlanta, was named Children's Healthcare of Atlanta's senior vice president, general counsel.[13]

Helping others is the fundamental concept at Children's Healthcare. The hard work and dedication of staff to others has enabled and inspired individuals like Jessica to make a difference as well. She has a great desire to work with autistic children in hopes of working toward a cure. Jessica was given an opportunity through the help and care of others. That opportunity led to another shot at life for her and instilled in her the desire to help others as well. She wants to offer that same generosity and opportunity to others who need it.

Making a Difference

Making a difference comes down to that inner voice that moves you to answer a need. Once you do that, everything else will fall into place. The people you meet, the lessons you learn about how to treat people, and the intrinsic and extrinsic rewards both you and your business will reap are unparalleled.

The best know that they are in a position to make a difference and that they have a responsibility to do just that. When we are successful, we offer others the chance to thrive as well. If you are reading this book, you probably want to improve some aspect of your personal or professional life. You may want to become a better communicator, negotiator, or leader. That has to start from within. And how you treat people will truly make or break your place in society. You have to invest in people so that people will invest in you, your cause, and your business.

Andrew Carnegie, one of the richest and most influential men in American history, once said, "I resolved to stop accumulating and begin the infinitely more serious and difficult task of wise distribution." If you are smart enough to earn big, you need to be smart enough to give big. This is evidenced by Bill Gates and Warren Buffett, two of the most successful and richest businessmen of our generation. Both have pledged at least half of their fortunes to charity either during their lives or after they pass away, and they have started recruiting others. So far, their Giving Pledge has recruited over fifty billionaires to give the majority of their wealth away. The concept behind this pledge is to recruit the richest and most successful people in the world to agree to give the majority of their wealth to charity for philanthropic purposes once they pass away.[14] These billionaires come from all different backgrounds and have made their money in many ways. But all of them have two things in common: they are the wealthiest of the wealthy, and they are philanthropists.

It is time to reimagine and refocus your life and business on an important lesson the best have learned throughout their careers: giving is just as important as getting.

6

Lead Like the Best

A leader is one who knows the way, shows the way,
and goes the way.
—JOHN C. MAXWELL

The best know how to lead and inspire teamwork among those who rely on them for direction. Many of the most successful people are in positions of power and leadership. Their responsibility is to take a group of different people from different backgrounds with various skill sets and talents and produce a cohesive and productive team that will have a successful result. But leading is about more than that. The best also inspire their team to become leaders in their own right. The best leaders understand that they cannot accomplish anything without a strong team. No successful company ever achieved its success without teamwork. It takes a dedicated and objective-oriented leader to guide and inspire a team of individuals so that they will be devoted to the end result and band together to reach it. This chapter will help you understand how to become that leader.

The Synergy Between Leaders and Their Teams

Anything can be accomplished when a leader works diligently to inspire his or her team to meet expectations and create results. Synergy is what happens when two or more people work together to produce results more quickly, easily, and efficiently than any one person could alone.

The best leaders of our time grasp the fundamental idea that a group of people working together toward a common goal is vastly more powerful than any single person trying to accomplish the same task. Effective leaders understand that their team should be able to work as a single strong unit and that their job as leader is to make that happen. Leaders should communicate short-term and long-term goals to their team so thoroughly that the team has a clear understanding of that vision and those goals and knows, without necessarily being told, how to achieve them. I call this the pulley system leader. Pulley system leaders are linked to their team so much that when they move in one direction, they pull their team with them, and the team reacts to that movement. And when a pulley system leader's team moves in one direction, the leader moves with them. This synergy causes the team not only to work together but also to remain connected with one another. This is the relationship great leaders develop with the people within their companies. They are so involved with one another in their vision and everyday operations that when one person pulls, everyone else feels it and reacts.

When leaders achieve true synergy with the people within their organization, anything is possible. This is evidenced by the reaction of Tulane University in New Orleans shortly after Hurricane Katrina, one of the most costly and deadliest hurricanes in U.S. history, hit the Gulf Coast in 2005. Doug Hertz, a member of the board for Tulane University and president and CEO of United Distributors in Smyrna, Georgia, discussed the aftermath of Katrina and how the school reacted. It had ravaged the university the weekend before the first day of classes; after it passed, Tulane was in shambles. It had no income because its students matriculated at other colleges until the campus was usable again. The faculty and staff had been evacuated along with the rest of New Orleans and could not return until the city was deemed safe. The tuition checks that the students had previously sent were ruined in the flood, along with most of the university records.

In the aftermath of the hurricane, the president of Tulane, Scott Cowen, had a difficult question to answer: How was he going to get the university open in six months? The future of the school was at stake, and he had to act quickly. First, he and his staff worked hard to place all students in other colleges and universities, which had opened their doors to these students, with Tulane absorbing the financial burden. He insisted to the board that the faculty and staff continue to receive their salaries and he brought them back to the school, housing them on cruise ships. The university went so far as to give loans to the faculty and staff so that they could begin rebuilding their homes.

Once President Cowen made his goals clear and showed that he was willing to support his staff in any way possible to help them reach those goals, they were eager to do whatever they could. They rebuilt and reorganized as a team and did everything from cleaning classrooms to rebuilding curricula from the destroyed documents and finding cost-effective measures to rebuild the university. Just five years after Katrina, Tulane had nearly reached its pre-Katrina enrollment numbers, evidencing a strong return from a terrible tragedy.[1]

This incredible recovery and quick reaction to a tragic situation would not have been possible without Scott Cowen's vision and the synergy of a strong team inspired by his foresight. Scott and his team had a seemingly impossible task on their hands: a natural disaster had destroyed an entire city, and Tulane was part of the catastrophic mess. There was no way any one person or small group of people could have made a difference on their own. But Scott and his faculty and staff focused on the power of synergy. Without a strong and dedicated team, Scott would not have been able to get Tulane up and running ever again.

With leadership and synergy, anything is possible. But it all starts from the top and moves down. It has to begin with the leader because it is the leader's responsibility to create that synergy. Former president of Towson University, James L. Fisher once said, "Leadership is the special quality which enables people to stand up and pull the rest of us over the horizon."[2] True leaders have the ability to create synergy and inspire others.

The Four Inherent Traits of a Leader

Although there are many different leadership styles and all successful leaders find a way to inspire others, all successful leaders share a common set of traits. Paul Voss, a professor in the Department of English at Georgia State University, believes that "the hundreds of books published each year under the category of 'leadership' actively testify to the importance of this term and the value we place on such actions. Leadership remains the dominant concern of business, governments, sports teams, families, clubs, and any other organization. For many generations, great minds have confronted the topic of leadership and explored the essential requirements for such behavior. Aristotle's *Nicomachean Ethics* provided an outline for individual leader based on the four cardinal, or hinge, virtues."[3]

Aristotle believed that all leadership is far more than charisma, popularity, or personal charm, and it is certainly more than the exercise of power or might. The great philosopher identified four characteristics necessary for human excellence:

Prudence: The intellect and decision-making power
Justice: Not playing favorites, no nepotism or cronyism, and creating fair procedure and policies that apply to all
Temperance: The harmony between reason and desire, that is, the ability to manage expectations and provide a work-life balance
Fortitude: Courage and the strength of character to overcome disappointment and setbacks

My own experience of leaders and leadership is very much in line with what Paul Voss shared with me based on his studies of Aristotle. Every good leader I have ever seen carries these four fundamental character traits: good sense (prudence), impartial integrity (justice), balanced determination (temperance), and resilient courage (fortitude).

Good Sense

All good leaders are not just smart, driven, and intelligent; they are also extremely practical and effective in their decision making. Certainly they are also passionate about their vision and their goals, but when it comes to executing on those goals, they have the good sense to implement them in the most efficient way, even if that means making some tough choices. Whether you are a quarterback and are getting blitzed by the defense or a CEO answering a difficult question live to the media or employees, the best react with good sense—and solutions. Leaders with good sense are also confident in their decisions and do not waver based on their last conversation. My brother was a fighter pilot before becoming a civilian pilot, and he said he would accelerate versus slow down in the heat of a moment. The same can be true in business. Often leaders have little time to weigh their options and the potential consequences before acting. These tough decisions often define a leader and inspire his team. Without good sense and the ability to make a hard call, a leader can become, unsure, confused, or stuck at a fork in the road.

Often leaders have little time to weigh their options and consequences before acting.

Impartial Integrity

A great leader takes the time to listen to others and treats them in an impartial and unbiased manner. But simply being impartial is not enough. Great leaders demonstrate their integrity and respect for their team by treating others with respect and implementing fair procedures and operating methods. The fallout from playing favorites can be monumental. It creates unhappiness and discomfort, and affects the overall morale of the team. Leaders are responsible for lifting their teams up and raising confidence and spirits. They create positive connections within the team verses using controlling tactics to gain more respect from their employees. Teams are more effective and engaged when they buy into their leader's philosophy. If the leader does not display impartial integrity, the chances that the entire team will buy into that vision are slim.

Balanced Determination

Healthy leaders understand the importance of a balance in their business and personal life and are determined to maintain this balance through all challenges and obstacles. Tony Conway, founder of A Legendary Event, understands the importance of balance: "I make appointments all day and every day. My life is appointment-to-appointment, meeting with potential clients, vendors, customers, and employees. So I have always made it a priority to schedule an appointment for my life as well. You have to have balance between work and life."[4] I believe that part of living a healthy and balanced life is getting sufficient rest, hydration, and nourishment while keeping exercise a priority. Clarity as to your priorities in life are imperative; with clarity, you determine what to say yes and no to. The result of that is balance.

Ernie Johnson Jr. also believes in the importance of balance and not losing track of the big picture. To remind himself of that, he recalls this story from his childhood:

> One of my favorite sports stories happened when I was nine years old. I am playing at Murphy Candler Park in Atlanta on a Little League team, and I am playing shortstop. This kid steps up to the plate and hits a line drive over my head, for a ground-rule double. After that play, the coach called us to the mound to talk strategy. When we ran back to our positions, we noticed that two outfielders were missing. Well, as it turns out, two of the players chasing the ball ended up finding a patch of blackberries right outside the outfield. They threw off their gear and started eating the berries.
>
> In life, we are so focused on the game. We need to step away from this. You don't get the chance every day to eat fresh wild blackberries.
>
> You have to remember to find a blackberry every day. There are blackberries all over the place in your life; you just have to look around and find them. You might even have to pick through some thorns to get to some blackberries, but those berries can be the most rewarding.[5]

The best know and understand the importance of creating a balanced life and stopping to eat the blackberries. But great leaders know that balance is also important in how they treat their team. Strong leaders keep morale high by providing comfortable structure and encouraging balance. They provide their team with the structure they need to succeed but also the comfort they need to be themselves and attend to their personal lives. Otherwise, the smart leaders know, they will burn out their best people. Successful leaders understand the importance of a balance between life and work and implement that balance not only in their own lives but also in their businesses and organizations to ensure that their team also achieves that balance.

Resilient Courage

Leaders who are truly special have more than courage and strength in the face of obstacles; they are also resilient and determined to reach their goals. Being brave is important, and most leaders are prepared for the fallout that their decisions can create, but the truly successful leaders are resilient and flexible enough to deal with those repercussions. It is easy to lead when times are good. But what happens when things get difficult? That is when resilient courage kicks in, and true leaders rise to the top.

Visionary Leadership

In addition to the four inherent traits that make leaders great, the vision that successful leaders maintain define them and separate them from others. All great leaders have a vision—a dream or idea of what they want the future to be—and they set goals to take themselves, their team, and their organization in that direction. Jack Welch, former chairman and CEO of General Electric, said, "Good business leaders create a vision, articulate the vision, passionately own the vision and relentlessly drive it to completion."[6]

Visionary leaders are forward thinking but also educated by experience. They are patient but determined to reach their goals without sacrificing the quality of their work. They are steadfast, deeply concerned for others, and compassionate; disciplined, focused, and sincere; and honest, trustworthy, authentic, and meticulous.

These characteristics are the basics that great leaders must have. But there are also less obvious character traits that leaders must have and things they must do to be truly visionary. A visionary leader focuses on things most people would not even consider as being vital to success.

Let's take a look at what you need to do to be a visionary leader.

Embrace and Initiate Innovation

Throughout my interviews with some of the most successful leaders in the world, a word that kept surfacing when I asked what qualities great leaders have was *innovation*. The concept of innovation is twofold. First and foremost, it is about being forward thinking and moving quickly in a direction before anyone else does. But even more important, innovation is about changing directions and reinventing as well. It starts with discovering a new and unique need and ends with redirecting your vision to stay ahead of the pack. Both skills are essential to being an innovative leader.

Having an innovative thought process is vital to your success as a leader. You must take a widely accepted notion or concept and play with it until you create something new and powerful. This is what great leaders do every day. They view the world differently from most other people. Where some of us may see a dead end, they see a waiting opportunity.

Joey Reiman has his own approach to creativity and innovation. He said:

> I am able to think better than others because I have a fluency of thought based on the ability to think like a child. To not be hampered by rolling eyeballs or what people might think. I try to think in an unconditioned environment in my head. Creativity is intelligence having fun. Anything unconditioned is creative. . . . Children . . . feel they have unlimited freedom. They are authentic until people tell them otherwise. Children love to discover and . . . wonder, living a life where you . . . discover something new every day. That is what innovation is all about. Picasso said it took him eighty years to become seven again. Innovative thinkers view the world like children because only then can they discover and dream.[7]

Joey's thought process is just one example of how innovative and creative ways of thinking allow leaders to reach the pinnacle of success in their business. Joey thinks for a living, and so do many other professionals. But the way Joey thinks is so innovative and unique that it makes him a visionary leader.

Innovation is not just about being different and unique in how you think or view life. Great leaders are also innovative in the face of difficult circumstances. One of the greatest innovators and examples of innovation in motion is Steve Jobs, founder of Apple. Jobs founded Apple with Steve Wozniak in 1976 and created and marketed one of the first lines of personal computers for the consumer market. He left Apple in 1984 after losing a difficult power struggle with the board of directors and went on to found NeXT, a computer company, and worked with Lucasfilm, which eventually led to the creation of Pixar

Animation Studios, where Jobs remained until 1996. At that time, Apple approached him and purchased NeXT, a sale that brought Jobs back to Apple and then to CEO, a position he held until August 2011.

When the board asked Jobs to leave the company he co-founded, he was faced with what could have been large and difficult obstacles to overcome. But by renewing his vision and changing his platform through innovation, he eventually made it back to the top and led the most innovative company in the world. Much of that came directly from Jobs's visionary leadership.

Innovation is a vital trait of all successful and visionary leaders. Whether it is the type of innovation that allows you to view things just a little bit differently than anyone else does or the innovation and know-how to reinvent and renew your business when difficult obstacles present themselves, innovation truly takes a good leader and transforms that person into a great one.

Keep Good Company

Many people say that you have to surround yourself with people who are smarter than you are, but in their next breath, these same people say, "I put people in place who would solve a problem in the same way that I would when I am not there." If you are committed to your vision, you have to have people around you who will execute according to that vision even when you aren't around. Arthur Blank believes that "a great leader hires people who would handle a situation the exact same way they would. . . . That is why you hire the people you hire."[8] There is a big difference between executing and leading. As the leader, you have to be confident that the people you surround yourself with will be true to your vision and solve problems accordingly.

Visionary leaders understand their limitations. I like to say that great leaders know their blind spots—they know what they don't know. As a leader, you have a great responsibility to understand your business and how it is run. But it is not always possible to understand every detail. That is why the person who holds the most powerful position in the world, the president of the United States, has a cabinet of successful and highly intelligent people who specialize in specific areas and can offer their advice.

I like to say that great leaders know their blind spots—they know what they don't know.

The best leaders surround themselves with the best team, including people who excel in areas where they do not. That is part of why they are strong leaders. They have a basic understanding of what they do not know and find people who do. They then designate responsibility and privilege to those people. The best leaders form a strong team and designate authority. No leader can do everything or be everywhere, so it is in this person's best interest and the best interest of his or her company to spread out the decision-making power.

You can't lead in a vacuum. Nothing of any significance can be done alone, and the smartest and most successful leaders understand that. As Bob Burg says, "There is no me without we."[9] Effective leaders must be able to bring people onto their team and enlist them into buying into and executing on their vision.

Stick to Your Core Values

Visionary leaders identify the core values that support their vision to ensure that they live by them. Patrick Lencioni, founder of the Table Group, a company that focuses on developing and implementing organizational effectiveness and teamwork within companies, and a best-selling author, has clearly identified values for his organization: humble, hungry, and smart. He and his staff align every decision with these fundamental concepts. Before an interview with a job applicant, he and his staff might discuss whether this person "is hungry, smart, and humble" and try to get clarity around this issue in the interview.[10] And at Southwest Airlines, the core values are humor, servant's heart, and "warrior spirit" (that is, an inner drive to win). Every decision made, every person hired, and every strategic and tactical act is anchored to those values.

Great leaders have clarity and alignment around their values and behave accordingly. In other words, they are intentional about their leadership. Properly drafted core values summarize who you are, what need you want to fulfill, and what direction you will move in to fulfill that need. Once you understand what your core values are, you can begin to inspire others to believe in those values and align their personal preferences with your ideas. Only then can you move in a direction that is beneficial to both you and your bottom line.

When it comes to creating and maintaining a vision, having core values in place that will help you do so is important. Those values should influence and shape not only who you are but also what your business will become. They also will serve as a way to inspire others to help you work toward your vision and build your future. That is why sticking to your core values is so vital to being a visionary leader. Focusing on maintaining these values through good times and not-so-good ones as your business grows will put you on the fast track to being one of the best.

Credit Your Team's Successes

To create a positive environment for your team, you have to give credit where credit is due. Great leaders do not take every success as their own; rather, they point people out and thank them for all they have done. No impossible task was ever accomplished without a team of hard-working individuals dedicated to a cause and vision. When leaders overcome the impossible, they make public who helped them along the way. If you don't acknowledge what your team does for you, they won't buy into you as a leader. A team needs to know that their work is appreciated and valued. Your team's effort, diligence, and accomplishments are what make you and your organization successful. Without them, you wouldn't make it far.

Great leaders both praise and reward their team. Certainly everyone appreciates being thanked and acknowledged, but actions do speak louder than words so it's important to reward your team's hard work. Peyton Manning, the starting quarterback for the Indianapolis Colts, a four-time Most Valuable Player of the NFL, and a Super Bowl champion, knows this well. In football, the quarterback is probably the most important position to any team's success. The players who protect the quarterback from getting hit by the other team are called the offensive line. Peyton Manning has one of the best offensive lines in the business, and that enables him to take the time he needs to make decisions in a fast-paced game. He has reached the pinnacle of success in his career and will be the first to tell anyone that he attributes much of his success to his team and the players standing in front of him and blocking. So what does Peyton Manning do? He buys expensive watches, custom suits, and various other gifts for his offensive linemen as a way to show his appreciation. Peyton may get much of the credit for his accomplishments, but without his team and an offensive line that works hard for him, he would not be able to complete a pass. And in 2010, Manning was the least sacked quarterback in the entire NFL, so his team is certainly holding up their end of the bargain.[11]

The best leaders ensure that credit for success is spread as widely as possible throughout the company. Great leaders understand that there are enough compliments, credit, and prosperity to go around. They know that they are there to drive the troops to success. The old saying, "The more you share, the more you have," is truly applicable here. If your team is happy, you will be far more likely to succeed. And much of that happiness will be derived by how appreciated your team feels. With a strong and motivated team, there is little you cannot accomplish, but with an underappreciated and undervalued team, there is little you can. To be a great leader, you have to spread the wealth, spread the love, spread the credit, and make sure that you thank, praise, and acknowledge everyone who made it possible.

Visionary leaders understand that it is their team's hard work, as much as their own, that helped propel them to the top. To achieve any vision, you have to meticulously and diligently build and maintain a strong and dedicated team. And this is done directly through your actions. Rewarding your team is not only about saying please and thank-you. It is about acknowledging their value openly by taking steps to improve their lives and showing your appreciation through your actions. You can reward your team with time, money, or anything in between, but whatever the case, happy and appreciated members of your team will give you the maximum they have to offer.

Happy and appreciated members of your team will give you the maximum they have to offer.

Sacrifice and Own Failure

Great leaders are selfless and take personal responsibility for failures. They put themselves in the line of fire, shielding their team, company, coworkers, and everyone else when things go wrong. If a sacrifice has to be made, a great leader will be the first to offer up what is necessary. To spread the fame and take the blame is a hallmark of effective leadership. This helps other people feel safe and draws the team closer together. If you are in a position of leadership, you are also the person everyone will look to when things go wrong. You will get much of the credit when your company succeeds, but you will also get the bulk of the blame when it fails. The failure may not be your fault; it could be the result of something you did not even have control over, for example. But that does not enter the calculation at all. Good leaders understand that sacrifice is part of what they do.

One of my clients and friends, Bobby Cox, retired as manager of the Atlanta Braves at the end of the 2010 season. He was with the Braves for over twenty-five years and was widely considered one of the top managers in the game. I bring him up here not because of his undeniable success as a Major League Baseball (MLB) manager, but because he sacrificed for his team probably more than any other manager. As the leader of his team, it was his responsibility to make the ultimate sacrifice: getting thrown out of the game.

Bobby was thrown out of baseball games more than any other manager because he would rather be the ejected one than one of his players. Bobby is a humble guy who rarely embraces the opportunity to be in the spotlight. But he has a vision for his team's success, so when it comes to saving his players and taking one for the team, he puts hesitancy aside and runs out of the dugout to make sure he takes the ejection instead of one of his players. Interestingly the number of Atlanta Braves who have been ejected since Bobby Cox took over is almost half of the MLB average. Because of Bobby's sacrifice for his team, the guys who pitch the fastballs and hit the home runs keep playing. Bobby understands the concept of sacrifice for the good of the team. He will be the first to tell you that he would take one for his players any day of the week. And the result is not just that his players continue to play. It is that they respect him, admire him, and buy into him as a leader.

Perhaps that is why the Atlanta Braves set an MLB record by winning the division title fourteen straight times under Bobby's leadership.

Leaders sacrifice. It is part of the job and part of the responsibility. Great leaders inspire their team to take a bullet, but they won't have to because their leader is the first in the line of fire. But it not just about the big sacrifices. It could be the sacrifice of time, stock in the company, or even the last sandwich at lunch. Regardless of how big or small the sacrifice, great leaders put their team first.

Work Toward a Better Future and Leave a Legacy

Visionary leaders see a better future and work to make it a reality. They focus on what they can do today to change the world tomorrow. It is not just about making a difference for one person on one day, though; it's about using their position of power to create something bigger, better, and lasting.

Mike Feinberg cofounded KIPP (Knowledge Is Power Program) because he had just such a vision. KIPP is a national group of public schools, predominantly based in underprivileged communities, that focus on preparing students for success in both college and the rest of life. Feinberg and Dave Levin, both former Teach for America participants, founded KIPP in 1994. After they finished their Teach for America commitment, they launched a curriculum for fifth graders in a public school in inner-city Houston, Texas. Feinberg developed KIPP Academy Houston into a charter school, while Levin went on to establish KIPP Academy New York in the South Bronx. As of 2011, seventeen years after the first school was founded, there are now ninety-nine KIPP schools in twenty states and the District of Columbia, home to over twenty-seven thousand students.

KIPP schools are charter schools that focus on accountability, more classroom time than other schools, and a strong culture of accomplishment. Most KIPP schools run from 7:30 A.M. to 5:00 P.M. Monday through Friday and 8:30 A.M. to 1:30 P.M. on select Saturdays (usually twice a month); middle school students also participate in a two- to three-week mandatory summer school, which includes extracurricular activities after school and on Saturdays. Over 80 percent of KIPP students are from low-income families and eligible for the federal free or reduced-price meals program, and 95 percent are African American or Latino. Nationally more than 90 percent of KIPP middle school students have gone on to college-preparatory high schools, and over 85 percent of KIPP alumni have gone on to college. Students are accepted in KIPP schools regardless of their prior academic record, conduct, or socioeconomic background.

When discussing KIPP, Mike said:

> I truly believe that change inspires change. Our job here is to make more actuals to prove the possibles. Since I have been doing this for sixteen years, I am old enough to see how some of the original KIPP kids have gone out, graduated from college, and are colleagues on our faculty. There are teachers, accountants, college counselors who all started in a KIPP program. That is the ultimate reward. That beats any paycheck. . . . A lot of the teachers I have met and led along the way have gone on to start their own schools, and watching them do what they do kind of makes me feel like a proud

grandparent because I know our school and our program inspired them to make a change in their own communities.[12]

Visionary leaders always find the opportunity to inspire change. They are compelled to make a difference and pass down the lessons they have learned to others in the hope that they too will do the same. In this way, they create a vast, powerful network of people who are trying to improve the world. A leader may not lead forever or be able to change the world forever, but what they can do is position themselves to leave a lasting legacy and help create other great leaders for generations to come.

The impact of great leaders may be hard to discern, but when we look back at the great leaders, from George Washington to Martin Luther King Jr., we can gain an understanding of the legacy they worked so hard to create during their time as a leader.

Inspire Others

To be a great leader, you have to inspire your team to believe in your vision. People buy into people before they buy into a vision or a company. People want to be inspired. In fact, there are a lot of people who will follow an inspiring leader even when the leader has no other qualities. If you have worked to develop the

Being inspiring means convincing people that your organization is going to change the world.

other traits of a leader, becoming an inspirational leader is usually just a matter of communicating clearly and with passion. Being inspiring means convincing people that your organization is going to change the world.

When Steve Jobs was starting Apple with Steve Wozniak, he was concerned with hiring the greatest and most inspirational CEO in the business. At the time, John Sculley was the CEO of Pepsi-Cola. Jobs met with him, looked him in the eye, and with a firm gaze, said, "Do you want to sell sugar water for the rest of your life, or do you want to come with me and change the world?" Sculley joined Apple and remained as CEO until 1993.[13] This is just one example of how visionary and innovative leaders can rock the universe with their inspirational leadership techniques. Being inspiring means showing people the big picture and helping them see their part in achieving the goal.

The best inspiration comes from stories of people who have achieved great feats. Stories can help you vividly illustrate what you are trying to communicate. Those that communicate on an emotional level leave an imprint much stronger than anything you can achieve through stating the facts. You can use true stories about your customers or business or even fables and myths. Learning to be inspiring is not easy, particularly for individuals lacking in charisma, but it can be learned. Take note of people who inspire you and analyze the way they communicate. Look for ways to passionately express your vision. Although there will always be room for improvement, a small investment in effort and awareness will significantly help you develop the ability to inspire others. Inspiration is contagious. Visionary leaders do not just inspire their team; they also inspire everyone around them, from customers, to potential clients, to other businesses with which they work, all the way down to the community at large. They literally touch everyone with their infectious enthusiasm.

Alana Shepherd's job is to offer inspiration to people in life's most difficult moments. She is the cofounder of the Shepherd Center of Atlanta, one of the top rehabilitation centers in the world and specializing in treating catastrophic spinal chord and brain injuries. Alana cofounded the Shepherd Center after her son, James, suffered a serious spinal injury during a trip to Brazil. There was nowhere in the South where he could receive treatment, so the family had to travel to Denver, Colorado, for James's extensive treatment program. Alana was a visionary and saw the need for a similar center in the South.

Alana is truly inspirational, and her bottom line is not monetary; she says, "At Shepherd we deal in hope." Shepherd takes a unique approach to rehabilitation. Alana explains that "everyone here looks at the patients who are injured and we don't feel bad for them; we think how they are going to get out of here after their hospitalization and rehab. They will be able to function in our society. They still may be paralyzed at the level of the injury, but they are not paralyzed from returning to society and living life at a high level." She also says, "It's not depressing here, it is inspirational.... They want to get stronger and do something better with what they have left. We inspire people, but people inspire us."

Once while Alana was touring the hospital, an ambulance arrived with a young man in it who had just been badly injured in an accident. Alana heard the hysterical mother say that his life was over and all his plans were ruined by the accident. Alana approached the mother and said, "Let me tell you something.

I want you to get the word *was* out of your vocabulary right now, because he is going to college, and he is going to get a job."[14]

Visionary leaders unlock the thriving potential of people around them by inspiring them. Great leaders fuel their team's ability to succeed. Inspiration fires people up and infuses a contagious excitement that propels them forward. When you inspire your team, they will buy into your vision and follow you to the end. Inspirational leaders motivate others to accomplish tasks they otherwise might not be able to accomplish. They start with leading by example and end with inspiring a reaction. When you can get your team to react to your leadership, you have won them over, and anything will be possible.

Conclusion

The best know how to lead. They understand the importance of surrounding themselves with a strong team and how to help their team accomplish more, succeed more, and reach for more. If you cannot inspire those around you, you will never be a true leader. But if you have the ability to take a group of people from different backgrounds and inspire that group to believe in your vision and follow you through good times and bad, then you will find that success will come your way. The best lead by example, but even more important, they lead through a constant determination and dedication to their work and their success. Each of us has the ability to become a great leader by focusing our time and energy on honing the ideas and concepts introduced in this chapter.

7

Build a Personal Brand

Good, better, best. Never rest until good be better and better best.
—Mother Goose

Being the best at what we do, no matter what that may be, is a goal we all work toward. We can always improve and always strive to be better. The best work diligently and meticulously to ensure that they are constantly reinventing themselves. They carry a unique position in life and strive to preserve their exceptional and inimitable qualities. Each of us has a unique set of skills and characteristics that we share with no one else. Sure, we may have commonalities with others, but our entire makeup is unlike anyone else's. These qualities are like fingerprints. We each have them, but they are completely different from person to person.

The best understand how to sell themselves like no other. They focus on their strengths and project those qualities into their careers. I have discussed numerous skills throughout this book that the best possess, but each also has a personal brand—the medium by which they wrap these skills up and deliver them to their clients. We all have to focus time and attention on our skills and find a way to ensure that our irreplaceable and defining traits are projected to the world.

You could master every skill that I have identified thus far, but if you can't create a marketable brand around the things that make you unique to separate yourself from everyone else, you will not succeed at being one of the best. The best consider how they will get people to buy into them, their ideas, and their business concept. That is what makes them special.

But building a strong brand is not just about finding and marketing your individuality. Certainly that is a big part of it, but it is also about finding what I call your DNA—your differentiator and accelerator. To succeed, you have to differentiate and accelerate. I always tell my clients they have to figure out how to differentiate themselves from others and then accelerate themselves to greatness. These are two separate yet connected ideas: find your angle, and drive yourself to success.

The Road Map to Branding Yourself

Branding yourself starts with three questions:

1. What is your passion?
2. What is your purpose and why?
3. What is your motivating force?

The best know the answer to these questions when they start their journey, and by the end, the rest of the world does as well.

What Is Your Passion?

Most successful businesspeople place emphasis on their own personal passion. They take that passion and turn it into something concrete. Steve Jobs gave us the iPod. Bill Gates gave us Windows. Sam Walton gave us Walmart. Barbara Walters gave us news. Jobs, Gates, Walton, and Walters all started with a single idea they were passionate about and used that passion to create something independent and new, separating their business or product from everything else in the marketplace.

The best take a passion and project it to the world. Butch Harmon is an author, a television personality, and a golf instructor widely considered to be the greatest in the world. He is best known for his work with Tiger Woods, but he has also served as the golf coach for Phil Mickelson, Ernie Els, Stewart Sink, Greg Norman, and numerous other professional golfers. Butch believes that "the best are passionate about what they do. It does not matter what industry they are in, they are simply passionate for their trade."[1] When the best brand their businesses and personalities, their passion is a big part of that brand. Your skill set may be similar to someone else's, but your passion is uniquely your own.

Jim Warner is an entrepreneur, author, and expert in helping others make the transition through change. He founded and eventually sold a large and successful software company in the 1980s and 1990s. He is also the founder of OnCourse International, a company that specializes in guiding both businesses in transition and individuals seeking personal transformation. Jim's work is "a blend of CEO coaching, executive team development, and succession planning." He believes that "the best have an infectious enthusiasm and passion for their work. They love what they do. I have worked hard to inspire and guide leaders to personal awareness, a passion for their life purpose, and authentic relationships at all levels. You have to create an understanding of 'what am I the best in the world at and what am I passionate about?' Creating personal awareness and combining it with a passionate life purpose is where the best begin."[2] This is the heart of personal branding. You have to be passionate about your brand and what it may represent. When you love what you do, it is not only infectious, but inspires others. In terms of personal branding, if you do not breathe life and love into your ideas and your business, you have no chance of differentiating yourself and succeeding.

The best know the value of passion. Scott Lindy, head program director for Star 94, an Atlanta-based radio station, tells a great story about a friend of his who owns a pizza restaurant in San Diego that demonstrates how passion for a business and an idea helps create a brand and leads to success. Competition among pizza restaurants is high in San Diego, and restaurants are constantly looking for ways to differentiate themselves. One way the local competition started doing so was by

> importing water from New York because they felt that is what made the best pizza dough. They advertised this New York pizza with Brooklyn water all over town. However, my friend was so passionate about making the perfect pizza, that he began researching every part of the pizza dough, from the water to the flour to the yeast, working to ensure that no stone went unturned in his endless quest to make the perfect pizza. He did not believe the answer was simply in the dough. He was literally knee deep in flour and he would plug numbers, research data, and consider every element in the process to master his trade. He was so passionate about the product his business created that he was nonstop

> and completely dedicated to creating the best slice of San Diego pizza possible. Even when people were importing water, he was studying the components of dough so he could create an amazing end result. This undying passion is what makes his pizza and his business so special.[3]

When competition is strong, it can be difficult to break into a market and differentiate yourself. But by focusing on the details and his passion for pizza, this restaurant owner was able to create a brand for himself and become very successful. If it were not for his passion and his dedication to branding himself as someone who would go the extra mile to make the best pizza, his business may have closed early on.

Passion inevitably leads to the quest for perfection. When you are passionate about your product, you want to work hard and generate the best product possible. Every journey toward perfection starts with a passion, and passion is also what the best use to power through obstacles, overcome adversity, and remain dedicated to their ideas when everyone tells them they have no chance. Dedication to perfecting your passion is an integral part of your brand and how you present yourself to the world. Part of branding yourself is showing the world that your business or your idea is unique and that there are characteristics that set it apart from the competition. Allow your passion to suffocate any fears you have of failing. You can't do that without passion. Dedication to perfecting your passion is an integral part of your brand.

What Is Your Purpose and Why?

Once you have clarity about your passion, it is important to understand what your purpose is. Why are you doing what you are doing? What need are you trying to fulfill? Joey Reiman, founder of BrightHouse, believes that "the difference between the most successful and the successful is that the most successful play on a higher plane. They are playing in the company of something greater: purpose. Their focus is not on the bottom line, but rather how their values line up with the world's issues. The greatest purpose is to search for ideas to inspire people and restore them."[4] It is important to live life with a purpose in mind, because it truly provides personal meaning. The same is true in business. You have to find your purpose and tie your business to that purpose. The best understand that true purpose is not about making money or getting wealthy. It is about finding an outstanding need that has not been addressed and fulfilling it. If you do that, success and wealth will likely be a natural side effect. But it has to start with a purpose. To properly brand yourself to be successful, you have to have directed passion. Your passion has to move you toward a finite goal, which is your purpose.

The best have a strong purpose behind their actions. They are not floating aimlessly through their industries. They know where they are going, and although they may not always be sure how they are going to get to their end result, they know without doubt why they are headed in a particular direction and what the result should be.

Mike Feinberg had purpose in founding KIPP:

> When we started KIPP, we did so to with great purpose. It is an issue of social injustice that right now, depending on the zip code of your birth, you have a greater or lesser chance of succeeding in school or life regardless of the effort that you put forth. This is so un-American. The

> expectations are different with higher- versus lower-income neighborhoods. We wanted to change society's beliefs and mind-sets. We started KIPP originally as two fifth-grade teachers to make a true lasting impact on kids. We made some lasting promises. It was about the kids and the promise that we made. Our purpose at KIPP was to ensure that everyone had a chance to be successful, no matter what their economic or social background.[5]

It is clear that Mike had a direct vision and purpose that he felt fit a need in society. There were no schools at the time like KIPP, and Mike's purposeful and direct desire to create something new drove his idea home. This is how he branded himself. Mike is now known as one of the cofounders of an institution that provides a unique and novel approach to education. Through his purpose, he has created his own brand.

Alana Shepherd, cofounder of the Shepherd Center, has a similar story. In 1973, her son James set out on a backpacking trip around the world after graduating from the University of Georgia. While bodysurfing off a beach in Rio de Janeiro, he was slammed to the ocean floor by a wave. James, twenty-two years old at the time, sustained a serious spinal cord injury that left him paralyzed from the neck down. After spending five weeks in a Brazilian hospital struggling to survive, he returned to the United States. His parents, Alana and Harold Shepherd, located a rehabilitation treatment facility in Colorado. After six months of intensive rehabilitation, James regained his ability to walk while using a cane and a leg brace. But the Shepherd family was frustrated with the lack of rehabilitation care options in the Southeast United States. Together with Dr. David Apple, the family founded the Shepherd Center in 1975 as a six-bed unit operating out of leased space in an Atlanta hospital.[6]

The Shepherds were obviously passionate about the need for a rehabilitation center in the Southeast because it touched their lives directly. But they took that passion and used it as a driving purpose to create the Shepherd Center, which is now among the top rehabilitation centers in the world, a powerful brand identity.

These are just two examples of passionate and purposeful vision. The best are passionate about their purpose, and they work to find a way to bring their passion to life and make their purpose a reality. Every success story—a new type of scholastic program in Houston and New York, a specialty spinal center that began in Atlanta, and all of the others—begins with a need and a passionate purpose. Your purpose is the driving force behind why you do what you do. Everyone has a different purpose, but regardless of what that purpose may be, to have a strong brand that people respect, value, and want to be a part of, it is imperative that you pursue your purpose in a way that sets both you and your business apart.

What Is Your Motivating Force?

Every life-changing and business-altering idea starts with a passionate individual following his or her inner motivating force. This is the inner force that moves people to distinction. We all have a motivating force that calls us to greatness and channels our enthusiasm and passion toward our purpose. The best know that passion alone is not enough. That passion needs a motivating force to steer it toward a purpose so that you achieve your desired result.

Exceptional thinkers across different industries have a motivating force that leads them to reinvent, recreate, and repurpose the norm. One of the examples of a strong motivating force can be seen in Ray Anderson, founder and chairman of Interface Inc., the world's largest manufacturer of modular carpet. Ray is known across environmental circles as the "greenest CEO in America" for his advanced and progressive stance on industrial ecology and sustainability. He is diligently working to make his company completely sustainable by 2020, a impressive goal because the carpet manufacturing business is widely considered to be one of the most environmentally hurtful industries in the world. But that did not deter Ray from believing there was a more environmentally considerate way to produce carpet. People thought his idea was a stretch, but his motivating force has kept him on the path to his ultimate goal. He has said:

> My motivation is a commitment to something beyond the bottom line. The bottom line is a wonderful end in itself. But the means to the end is what is important. The companies that I admire the most have a clearly stated mission that goes beyond the bottom line—a higher purpose. That purpose is a commitment to excellence and a commitment to customer intimacy. At Interface Inc., I had read a book by Paul Hawken called *The Ecology of Commerce*, where he said the biosphere is in decline and the biggest culprit is business and industry, and how we take from the earth and what we use ends up as waste. This is a take, make, and waste industrial system. It prevails today all over the world. There is only one institution that can change that—the same one responsible for it. If businesses

> don't change, then it is just a matter a time before we cause a global collapse. The big leveler is us: businesses. We made a significant commitment to take Interface Inc. and make an impact through progress and working toward a sustainable company. We have seen other companies following along.
>
> Every product we produce will have an environmental disclosure. Total transparency. We tell on the product what is in the product and where it came from. Our goal is to expose the footprint and the environmental impact. We have challenged all industries to be conscious and more transparent. This exercise creates a platform to influence others. Throughout Interface Inc. there is an understanding that we are working for a higher purpose.[7]

This is how the best brands win, by possessing a strong motivational force. We all want to make a difference in the world and leave a mark that lasts well after we are gone. It is not easy. The best of the best focus on creating a brand and then use it to influence the way people think. They look to differentiate themselves from the pack and find a need that only their vision can fulfill.

Your unique motivation is part of what defines your brand.

Your unique motivation is part of what defines your brand. Many people will buy carpet from Ray instead of some other carpet manufacturer because his company is environmentally conscious and seeks to reduce its carbon footprint. His motivating factor is also a huge differentiator and part of his brand. Why you do what you do can be just as important as what you do. And by combining your passion with a steadfast purpose and fueling it with your motivational force, you create a strong brand for both yourself and your business.

What Is Your DNA?

By now, you should have a pretty good understanding of how the best create an individual brand for themselves. However, it is not enough to be passionate, purposeful, and motivated. The best also understand that just as you would differentiate products and ideas, you need to differentiate yourself. Embrace the qualities that make you uniquely you, and they will help you stand out and also help make you strong. This is your DNA—the things that differentiate you and help you accelerate beyond the rest. Think about the most successful people in the world. They embrace what makes them different and use those differentiating factors to blaze new trails and move forward. They accelerate both themselves and their ideas toward success.

The best differentiate themselves in many ways. Cecil Beaton, an Academy Award–winning stage and costume designer, once said, "Be daring, be different, be impractical, be anything that will assert integrity of purpose and imaginative vision against the play-it-safers, the creatures of the commonplace, the slaves of the ordinary."[8] To truly brand yourself, you have to differentiate yourself from the common, the habitual, and the everyday. You have to become the rare, the special, and the exceptional. And each of us has the ability to do that.

Throughout my interviews with some of the most successful people in the world, I learned a lot about their unique abilities to differentiate themselves throughout their respective industries. I also learned how their own perspectives on life have improved both their personal and professional lives in numerous ways. I will let them speak for themselves. Here are some of the best commenting on the ways they have differentiated themselves in their own respective industries and how their ways of viewing the world have enriched their lives.

Joe Theismann on Defeat

> We were in the midst of the 1985 season, and it was a bad one. We lost games we should have won. We got ready to play the Giants one night, and it was a typical Redskins/Giants game, more like a street fight. Coach called a play, and within seconds of the ball being hiked, I suffered a terrible injury to my leg. It was a compound open fracture of the right leg. Being an athlete, you know your body; you know the difference between injured and hurt. Some guys use hurt as an excuse, but you learn the difference. I was quickly placed on a gurney and in an ambulance. My bones were sticking out of my leg, and once I arrived at the hospital, I demanded they put me in front of a television so I could watch the game. Once I found out we won, I said I was fine to go into surgery.
>
> From this experience, I learned that the best recover from adversity because they don't accept defeat—mental, emotional, or even physical. The term *defeat* doesn't exist. There are challenges but not defeat. I have never had a defeat, only educational experiences that haven't gone my way that I

> have learned from. When something doesn't go right, there is an immediate opportunity to learn about you.
>
> My leg was broken, and I came to find out all the material things I held sacred were not what mattered. You have to embrace the challenge and move forward with who you are. By nature, we will blame other people. What separates the masses and those who are exceptional is an honest assessment of who they are and the ability to understand you simply cannot be defeated.[9]

What sets Joe apart from other people and athletes is that no matter what the circumstances are, defeat is not an option. Although his football career ended, Joe began a new career as a sportscaster.

In life, we all face difficult times that can be overwhelming. But what makes Joe different is that he just won't give up.

Doug Hertz on Learning

> You learn with every new opportunity, different circumstances, different environments, and different successes and failures. Anyone who has been extremely successful has had some failures. You have to learn from those—chalk them up to learning experiences. So then the chances of doing that again are small, and you improve your chances of success. Look back and analyze: What happened to make this work? What happened to keep it from being successful? What can I learn from this experience?[10]

Failure happens to everyone, and most people move on. Unfortunately, not everyone has the wisdom to look at their failures and analyze them to see what they can learn from the experience. For Doug, this is an important part of how he learns, and it makes him different from all those who face failure and then just try to forget about it.

Ray Anderson on Competiveness

> Nothing fails like success. When you find a successful combination and you settle into it, you have trouble just around the corner. Don't get too comfortable. When you get complacent, you are done.... In every organization . . . you have to constantly reinvent yourself. You have to anticipate things. You have always got to be thinking about how you can reform before the storm occurs. It starts with being competitive and never stopping.[11]

Lots of companies start out competitively but grow complacent once they reach a certain level of success. When you are at the peak of success and your share price is soaring, it's easy to forget about all the people and organizations ready to watch you fail so that they can take your place. Ray understands this, so for him, it is vital to keep tapping into his competitive spirit. We all want to succeed. But a truly competitive nature is what differentiates Ray, and many other successful people and companies, from the rest.

Joey Reiman on Personal Improvement

> My wife came from Los Angeles and a divorced family. I came from a dysfunctional family in New York. But we were (and are) so in love. One day before we got engaged, we talked about how we would keep this fire going and came up with this wild idea to go to the best marriage psychologist

> we could find. We found a doctor named Arthur Cohen. We went to him and told him, "We are not here to save our marriage; we are here to savor our marriage." We learned lessons from him and used his office as a studio for our own minds, hearts, and souls. Even though we did not have problems in our marriage, we felt that if we could constantly work to improve ourselves, we would never have problems with our marriage. . . . To this day, we still have appointments with Dr. Cohen. We choose to go when things are good so we don't have to go when it is too late.[12]

Most people go to a therapist to work through problems, but Joey and his wife went to a therapist to prevent problems. For both of them, having a strong and loving relationship wasn't enough. They knew they would have to work hard to keep it that way and that they couldn't become complacent about their happiness. This is a unique way to look at self-improvement.

Stedman Graham on Clarity

> One of the keys to differentiating yourself is clarity. You have to understand what you do well. You have to be authentic. You have to be very clear about where you are going, how you are going to get there, and understand what steps will get you there. How do you align the pieces of the puzzle? You have to be prepared and clear with your vision. You have to be mission driven, and you have to work on the groundwork to create a strong clarity for your vision.[13]

For Stedman Graham, differentiating himself from the competition means having a clear purpose. This is because he knows that if you aren't driven and purposeful, you will never be successful. The world is full of smart people with great ideas, but only those who have a clear path and purpose succeed. That clarity sets them apart and drives them to success that for so many others is just a pipe dream.

Jim Warner on Taking Risks

> You have to have a willingness to take on calculated risks. It is important to understand that there is no sure thing, but have a willingness to push the envelope, while also considering a strategy to minimize the potential for failure or the impact of failure. Take a risk, but strategize and plan on the front end for whatever your desired outcome will be. Opportunities are knocking, and if you aren't prepared or not willing to invest the time on the front end to see where it will lead you, you have no chance.[14]

For Jim Warner, an important part of being successful is not being afraid to take risks. He knows that while some may pan out, others won't, but jumping in and taking the chance is the only way to find out for himself. Not taking risks means letting potential opportunities pass by and for Jim, that is unacceptable. Risk taking is one part of Jim's personal brand.

Alana Shepherd on Customer Service

> When it comes to our patients, I think that you have to address their feelings and any problems they may have head-on. You don't try to bury them. Patients can be

> unhappy because of what happened to them, but not because of the care they are receiving. If they are upset, I immediately tell them, "I am so sorry this is not going well for you," and then I quickly ask how we can make it better. I have more crows' feathers hanging out of my teeth than anyone else. It is not so bad eating crows' feathers; it becomes rather tasty at the end of the day.[15]

Alana Shepherd believes that what sets the Shepherd Center apart from some other rehabilitation facilities is its approach to customer service. She knows that it is important not only to be compassionate and help the patients but also to be forthright, frank, and honest with them as well, addressing their unhappiness and their issues as they arise. Having this approach to customer service as an ingrained part of her own personal brand and the Shepherd Center's brand as well has clearly been one of the factors in their success.

Mike Feinberg on Evolving

> Being successful and evolving is really just about having a balanced perspective, about continuing to do what we always have done that has worked for us, while also keeping an eye out to get better and improve. You have to be humble, but you also have to keep learning and continue looking for more great people to add to the team, so that you can improve the quality of the product and evolve into something better.[16]

Mike Feinberg is an evolution advocate. He knows that it's easy to stagnate when you've reached success and that many people do. He differentiates himself by always looking for new ways to evolve and improve himself, KIPP schools, and his team.

Jim Warner on Personal Reflection

> I strive to take three to four weeks a year for reflection time or attending mind-bending seminars, trainings, or experiences. I also have a personal advisory board that both watches my back and challenges me to push the envelope. Also, I'm becoming more committed to awareness than excellence. The more disciplined, conscious, and aware I become, the more excellence seems to flow through me versus my trying to create it myself. I'm working hard on the transition from "Life happens by me," to "Life happens through me." And that begins with personal reflection of who I am and what I can become.[17]

Personal reflection helps Jim be active about his fate. By honestly reflecting on who he is and who he wants to be, and taking steps to change himself and his behaviors, he controls his life in a way that many others do not and cannot. As Jim eloquently puts it, so many people let life happen to them, not through them. Taking control of himself and his life through personal reflection makes him uniquely one of the best.

Ernie Johnson Jr. on Priorities

> During every on-air broadcast of our show, I always find a few seconds to tug on my cufflinks. It signals to my family at home that "I love you and I am thinking about you." It is something I have to deal with all of the time. At one point

> in my life, the light bulb went on, and I quickly realized that there is more to my life than what I am allowing to happen, and that is when it all changed, and I came to the understanding that there are plans that are greater than mine. That is what opens your eyes to where your priorities are in life. Work is important, but it will not define who I am. It is what I do, it's not who I am. My family is who I am.[18]

Ernie Johnson Jr. believes that business should never be your only priority or even your highest priority, and he diligently works to maintain balance in his life. He understands that there are people and things that are even more important than his career, and he is unwilling to sacrifice time spent with those he loves for the sake of things he wants to obtain. This is a strong part of Ernie's identity and brand and actually helps him to maintain his success because taking time away from work keeps him happy and allows him to infuse his work with new energy.

The Road to Success

The examples are plentiful. The best brand themselves by differentiating the way they look at life. The most successful people in the world view life, both personally and professionally, just a little differently than everyone else does. But it does not stop there. Differentiating yourself and your views is just one piece of your DNA. The best also accelerate their message. They are full speed ahead in the way that they brand themselves and their business.

Joey Reiman has numerous examples from his life and work that demonstrate how the best accelerate their message and ideas. Whether he was pitching Del Taco or Cadillac, Joey has always focused on propelling his ideas forward by presenting his vision in a unique and innovative fashion. This can be seen in how he pitched a tourism account: "When we were pitching an account to the head of tourism for the Bahamas, we took our entire office and turned it into a beach. We brought in hundreds of pounds of sand and put sand throughout the entire office. We set up a volleyball net in the conference room and had all of our employees show up to work wearing bathing suits and Hawaiian shirts."

Accelerating your position in the market is vital to success in business. It comes down to figuring out how to gain steam and how to gain the support of your market. It is not an easy task, but once you understand how to drive your ideas and business, the sky is the limit. To accelerate your business, you also have to accelerate your persona, because people buy into people before they buy into a concept or product. The easiest way to accelerate your persona is through honing the skills discussed in this book. Once you refine those abilities, the rest will fall into place.

Go Be the Best

I hope that the wisdom in the stories and examples in this book has left you feeling inspired, enlightened, and prepared to join the ranks of the best. As Samuel Johnson said, "People need to be reminded, not instructed," and I have set down the stories in this book to remind you that you have what it takes to be the best. You just need to hone and develop certain skills. We all can and should develop. Even the best have room for growth.

Now that you know exactly what it takes to be the best and what traits, skills, and characteristics the best share, you can begin to develop them within yourself to elicit a positive change in your life and give you clarity regarding your personal vision. Karl Rove said to me when he was talking about his experiences in Washington as George W. Bush's right-hand man in the White House, "You can't find out who you are or what you believe when you arrive at the White House. You better have known the answer to that question before you get there." This same is true for all career paths. If you are not clear about your identity, your brand, and your vision before you start climbing the ladder of success, you won't have a foundation to keep you going in the face of the obstacles that will inevitably stand between you and your goal.

There are numerous tools and strategies you can implement to improve the way you operate. The best understand the power of these strategies and have diligently worked every day of their professional careers to become top-notch communicators, negotiators, givers, leaders, and branders. Success does not happen overnight, but it is within reach. The resources are in front of you, and the knowledge is there. You have gained insight from some of the most influential thinkers of our time. Now it is time for you to begin implementing it into your own life.

I hope that this book has helped give you the foundation you need to be successful in your own area, whatever that may be. Just remember, above all else, that no matter what you do, make it your business to be in the business of being the best.

Notes

Chapter One

1. Michigan State Men's Basketball, retrieved May 4, 2011, from www.msuspartans.com/sports/m-baskbl/mtt/izzo_tom00.html#.
2. Interview with Tony Conway, Nov. 2, 2010.
3. Interview with Roger Staubach, June 2010.
4. Retrieved May 4, 2011, from www.pro-football-reference.com/players/S/SandBa00.htm?redir.
5. Interview with John Smoltz, Oct. 3, 2010.
6. Interview with Arthur Blank, Oct. 10, 2010.
7. Interview with Blank.

Chapter Two

1. Interview with Mark Kanov, Feb. 12, 2011.
2. Interview with Joey Reiman, Dec. 13, 2011.
3. Interview with Reiman.
4. CNN.Com retrieved May 4, 2011, from http://articles.cnn.com/2006-08-30/justice/jeffs.arrest_1_fugitive-polygamist-warren-steed-jeffs-polygamist-leader?_s=PM:LAW.
5. Anthony D'Angelo, www.brainyquote.com, Jan. 23, 2011.
6. TED.com, retrieved May 4, 2011, from http://www.ted.com/talks/william_ury.html.

Chapter Three

1. Interview with Joey Reiman, Dec. 13, 2011.
2. Interview with Arthur Blank, Oct. 10, 2010.
3. Interview with Tony Conway. Nov. 2, 2010.
4. Interview with Ernie Johnson Jr., Dec. 18, 2010.
5. B. Burg and J. D. Mann, *The Go-Giver: A Little Story About a Powerful Business Idea* (New York: Penguin, 2007).
6. Interview with Bob Burg, Dec. 12, 2010.
7. Interview with Reiman.
8. Interview with Johnson.
9. Interview with Scott Lindy, Jan. 10, 2011.
10. Interview with Conway.
11. N. Mandela, retrieved Feb. 11, 2011, http://thinkexist.com/quotation/as_a_leader-i_have_always_endeavored_to_listen_to/148828.html.
12. Interview with Conway.
13. L. V. Gerstner Jr., *Who Says Elephants Can't Dance? Inside IBM's Historic Turnaround* (New York: Collins, 2002).
14. Interview with Joe Theismann, Dec. 15, 2010.

Chapter Four

1. Interview with Ernie Johnson Jr., Dec. 18, 2010.
2. Interview with Bob Burg, Dec. 12, 2010.
3. Interview with Edie Fraser, Jan. 11, 2011.
4. Interview with Fraser.
5. Interview with Burg.
6. V Foundation, retrieved May 6, 2011, from http://www.jimmyv.org/.
7. V Foundation, retrieved May 6, 2011, http://www.jimmyv.org/share-your-story/memories-of-jim.html.
8. Interview with Johnson.

Chapter Five

1. Interview with Bob Burg, Dec. 12, 2010.
2. Retrieved July 9, 2011, from www.stedmangraham.com.
3. Interview with Stedman Graham, Dec. 16, 2010.

4. Interview with Ernie Johnson Jr., Dec. 18, 2010.
5. Interview with Johnson.
6. Interview with Graham.
7. "Job Openings at CECP," retrieved July 9, 2011, from http://www.corporatephilanthropy.org/about-cecp/careers.html.
8. Committee Encouraging Corporate Philanthropy, retrieved from http://www.corporatephilanthropy.org/.
9. "Give a Day, Get a Disney Day," HandsOn Network, http://www.handsonnetwork.org/Disney/training.
10. Children's Healthcare of Atlanta, retrieved May 14, 2011, from http://www.choa.org/Childrens-Hospital-Services/Cancer-and-Blood-Disorders.
11. Interview with Donna Hyland, Dec. 19, 2010.
12. Interview with Hyland.
13. Interview with Hyland.
14. The Giving Pledge, retrieved May 6, 2011, from http://givingpledge.org/.

Chapter Six

1. Interview with Doug Hertz, Jan. 14, 2011.
2. Retrieved July 9, 2011, from www.thinkexist.com.
3. Interview with Paul Voss, Dec. 12, 2010.
4. Interview with Tony Conway, Nov. 2, 2010.
5. Interview with Ernie Johnson Jr., Dec. 18, 2010.
6. BrainyQuote, retrieved May 6, 2011, from http://www.brainyquote.com/quotes/authors/j/jack_welch.html.
7. Interview with Joey Reiman, Dec. 13, 2011.
8. Interview with Arthur Blank, Oct. 10, 2010.
9. Interview with Bob Burg, Dec. 12, 2010.
10. Interview with Patrick Lencioni, Mar. 12, 2011.
11. T. Reynolds, "Manning's Colts Get the Goods," *New York Post*, Feb. 5, 2010, http://www.nypost.com/p/sports/more_sports/manning_men_get_the_goods_AOZhv7F9g2uIvyXXiIVuzJ.
12. Interview with Mike Feinberg, Jan. 15, 2011.

13. "Steve Jobs," Wikipedia, retrieved May 6, 2011, from http://en.wikipedia.org/wiki/Steve_Jobs.
14. Interview with Alana Shepherd, Jan. 12, 2011.

Chapter Seven

1. Interview with Butch Harmon, Jan. 15, 2011.
2. Interview with Jim Warner, Feb. 12, 2011.
3. Interview with Scott Lindy, Jan. 10, 2011.
4. Interview with Joey Reiman, Dec. 13, 2011.
5. Interview with Mike Feinberg, Jan. 15, 2011.
6. Interview with Alana Shepherd, Jan. 12, 2011.
7. Interview with Ray Anderson, Feb. 22, 2011.
8. Retrieved July 9, 2011, from www.thinkexist.com.
9. Interview with Joe Theismann, Dec. 15, 2010.
10. Interview with Doug Hertz, Jan. 14, 2011.
11. Interview with Anderson.
12. Interview with Reiman.
13. Interview with Stedman Graham, Dec. 16, 2010.
14. Interview with Jim Warner, Feb. 12, 2011.
15. Interview with Shepherd.
16. Interview with Feinberg.
17. Interview with Warner.
18. Interview with Ernie Johnson Jr., Dec. 18, 2010.

Acknowledgments

I owe enormous thanks to many others over the course of writing this book.

Thanks to all my clients for allowing me to contribute to your success and for the honor of being beside you for your career: your wins, loses, hirings, firings, deals, and awards. Throughout our years together, I have helped you maximize your window of time on a world stage, but we have learned from each other all along the way, and I am very grateful.

Thank to my wonderful husband, Fred Fletcher, and our precious miracles (our three daughters) for your support of this book. Thanks to my wonderful parents, Mary and Ken West; and my twin big brothers, Jim and John, who beat me up and made me tougher.

This book wouldn't have been written without the commitment of Justin Spizman, a magical writer, attorney, friend, and "half full" thinker who helped wrap the interviews and my thoughts into what you are reading today and made the process of pulling it together fun. I appreciate you dearly and thank you so much for your skill, wisdom, and passion.

Thank you to Jossey-Bass and my literary agent, John Willig. I appreciate your knowledge and guidance.

So many wonderful people were kind enough to answer the questions that I posed to them because I knew that readers would benefit from their answers. I interviewed businesspeople from Arthur Blank to Roger Staubach to so many others who have never made a living hitting, throwing, or catching a ball. You are busy, you get lots of requests, and I am grateful you accepted mine. Your words, wisdom, experiences, and insight are so helpful to those I wrote the book for. Thank you from the bottom of my heart.

Thank you to all of the other people I have been so fortunate to connect with over the years. These experiences, both grand and humble, have contributed to the insights that I have set out in this book.

At the core, I live to help and inspire others. I am not an emergency room doctor, so I humbly admit my level of helping others should be put in perspective. But it is my passion to take thousands of unique experiences with the best of the best, insert my perspective into them, and share them in a way that connects with you: your world, your needs, your wants, and your vision for your life. The people I have acknowledged here are the core of the thread that weaves through the pages of this book. I am grateful to them all, and I again appreciate their kindness, positive human energy, and passion for giving and inspiring others to be their best.

About the Author

Molly Fletcher, whom CNN has referred to as "the female Jerry McGuire," has worked with and represented hundreds of Major League Baseball stars, National Basketball Association coaches, PGA and LPGA golfers, National Collegiate Athletic Association coaches, and media personalities. She began her career in the sports business representing a handful of athletes and coaches. By 2010, she represented 250 professional athletes and coaches and had acquired a team of sports agents and marketing executives to help support the clients.

Molly speaks throughout the country in an effort to improve her audience's ability to deliver more value to their company, team, partners, clients, and selves. She has been featured extensively in national and local media, including CNN, ESPN, the *Wall Street Journal*, *Atlanta Journal and Constitution*, *Sports Illustrated*, *USA Today*, and *Washington Post*. In 2008, she wrote, *Your Dream Job Game Plan: Five Tools for Becoming Your Own Career Agent*, a tactical guide to building and managing relationships in an effort to advance into the business world.

Molly graduated from Michigan State University, where she competed on the women's tennis team all four years, captaining the team her senior year. She is married to Fred Fletcher and is the mother of three daughters, including a set of twins.

Molly would love to hear from you. Please contact her at www.mollyfletcher.com or follow her on Twitter via @molly fletcher.

Index